EKADASHI
The Eleventh Day
Tuning Inner Waters to the Cosmic Ocean

A Yogic Journey Through Sacred Ekadashis. Exploring the Origins, Vedic Stories, Lunar Fasting, and Divine Mantras — A Spiritual Guide Rooted in Sanatana Dharma.

Author:
Sourav Singh

"Emptiness is not absence; it is sacred presence"

Copyright Page

Title: *Ekadashi – The Eleventh Day: Tuning Inner Waters to the Cosmic Ocean*
Author: Sourav Singh
Year of Publication: 2025
ISBN (Paperback): 978-93-342-8719-6
ISBN (eBook): 978-93-342-9746-1
Publisher: Self-published

This work represents a spiritual and cultural synthesis, drawing upon sacred Hindu scriptures, traditional wisdom, and contemplative insight. It is intended for devotional reading, spiritual reflection, and educational purposes.

Cover Composition and formatting: Sourav Singh
Printed: Worldwide

"The journey inward begins in stillness"

✿ Dedication

(A whispering breeze across the hidden depths of the soul)

To those who seek clarity beyond the surface of everyday life, who yearn to quiet the noise of the world and listen to the subtle whispers of the inner self. May the ancient practice of Ekadashi open a door to deeper understanding, offering purification and enlightenment on the journey toward self-realization.

"Every breath is a doorway to the Infinite"

✿ Disclaimer

The content in *Ekadashi: The Eleventh Day – Tuning Inner Waters to the Cosmic Ocean* is for informational, educational, and spiritual growth purposes only. It offers insights into Ekadashi fasting, spiritual growth, Vedic teachings, lunar fasting, self-realization, meditation practices, and holistic health, rooted in traditional Sanatana Dharma. This book is not a substitute for professional medical or psychological advice. Please consult a qualified healthcare provider before making any dietary or lifestyle changes, particularly for individuals with pre-existing conditions or under medical care.

"As the moon waxes and wanes, so too the mind. Align with its rhythm, and you will know peace"

Contents

Preface

A Journey to the Inner Waters of Consciousness

🏵 A Sacred Invitation to Ekadashi

There are days in life when the ordinary dissolves, and the divine whispers through the silence. Ekadashi is one such day—a portal in time, a sacred current flowing within the vast cosmic ocean. It is not merely a fast but a tuning of our inner waters to the divine rhythm of the universe.

Since ancient times, sages, seekers, and householders alike have revered Ekadashi Vrata as an opportunity for self-purification, inner transformation, and spiritual awakening. It is a day when the body, the mind, and the soul realign, stepping beyond mundane existence into the realm of clarity, devotion, and transcendence.

To fast on Ekadashi is not merely to abstain from food—it is to partake in a higher nourishment, a subtler energy that feeds the spirit rather than the stomach. It is an invitation to experience a lighter body, a clearer mind, and a deeply awakened heart.

What is this Book About?

This book is an offering—a humble yet profound guide to the sacred wisdom of Ekadashi. It is for devotees, seekers, and researchers alike—whether you are observing this Vrata for spiritual merit, health benefits, or scholarly exploration.

Each chapter is woven with:

The Origin Stories – Mystical narrations from ancient scriptures, revealing the divine past of each Ekadashi.

Sacred Mantras & Shlokas – Prayers and invocations to harmonize consciousness with Lord Vishnu's divine presence.

Vishnu Visualization & Meditation – Guided techniques, integrating the cosmic energy of fasting into spiritual practice.

Sacred Rituals & Observances – A complete step-by-step guide on how to observe each Ekadashi with devotion, purity, and auspiciousness.

Through these chapters, you will discover that Ekadashi is not just a fast, but a cosmic alignment—a sacred tuning between individual consciousness and the eternal divine current.

ॐ The Call of the Eleventh Day

The word Ekadashi (Sanskrit: एकादशी) comes from "Eka" (one) and "Dashi" (ten)—the eleventh lunar day. It is a moment of great energetic shift in the subtle realms. Ancient texts describe Ekadashi as a divine threshold, where the dense pull of material existence begins to loosen its grip, allowing the soul to rise effortlessly toward spiritual light.

Even modern science offers a glimpse into this truth. Research on lunar rhythms, bioenergetics, and fasting shows that the 11th lunar day is uniquely aligned with the body's natural detox cycles. The ancient wisdom of Ekadashi was not superstition—it was a conscious alignment with the cosmic flow.

What Happens on Ekadashi?

- The moon's gravitational pull is at a specific resonance, subtly affecting the body's water content and cellular rhythms.
- Digestion slows down naturally, making fasting easier and more beneficial.
- The mind experiences heightened clarity, making it a powerful day for prayer and meditation.
- Spiritual vibrations are intensified—chanting Vishnu's name on this day yields a

thousandfold benefit.

This is why sages recommended fasting, chanting, and silence—it allows spiritual energies to unfold effortlessly.

✿ Ekadashi: A Universal Gift

For yogis, it is a time to refine prana (life force) and dhyana (meditation).

For scientists, it is an exploration of fasting and mind-body harmony.

For everyone, it is an opportunity to reset, rejuvenate, and realign with the higher self.

As you turn these pages, may you experience the deeper wisdom behind Ekadashi, beyond mere ritual, into the realm of cosmic truth and inner transformation.

May this book be your companion on this sacred journey.

On this day, may your heart awaken like a lotus at dawn.

May your consciousness merge with the divine waters of Vishnu's grace.

May Ekadashi illuminate your path—now and forever.

Chapter 1 — The Sacred Pulse of Time: Discovering the Meaning of Ekadashi 🌿

Exploring the Rhythmic Wisdom of Conscious Fasting and Cosmic Alignment

---

🏵 Time as Sacred Breath

In the vast cosmic rhythm, time is not measured merely in seconds or hours; it is breathed — like a living presence — by the Divine itself.
Every phase of the moon, every movement of the stars, and every cycle of days is seen in Sanatana Dharma as a vibration, a song, a living pulse of consciousness.

Within this sacred calendar, the day called Ekadashi — the eleventh lunar day — gleams as one of the most potent alignments of human spirit with divine time.

The sages of Bharatavarsha (India) did not merely calculate time; they listened to it. They realized that certain days were spiritually electric, where even a small effort could yield immense purification.

🌷 The Cosmic Mathematics of Ekadashi

In the simple yet profound understanding of Vedic timekeeping:

- The moon waxes (Shukla Paksha) and wanes (Krishna Paksha) every month.
- Each phase has 15 tithis (lunar days).
- The 11th tithi of both waxing and waning cycles is revered as Ekadashi.

◆ **Eka** means "one,"
◆ **Dashi** means "ten" –
Thus, Ekadashi literally means "the eleventh."

🌙 Astronomically, it is observed that on Ekadashi days, the gravitational effects of the moon have a unique influence on the human body's water composition, affecting mind stability, emotional equilibrium, and energetic flow.

Ancient Insight:

The Rishis (Sages) recognized that the subtle pranic (life force) tides inside us resonate closely with lunar rhythms.
Fasting on Ekadashi reduces physical burden.

A Personal Journey into the Mystery of Ekadashi: A True Story

(How I Discovered the Eleventh Day Was Already Within Me)

There was a time in my life when, every now and then, I would wake up feeling unusually quiet inside. It wasn't sadness, and it wasn't fatigue—it was something subtler, a stillness. On these days, I didn't feel like eating anything. It wasn't a decision, just a natural feeling from within. Food, even my favorite dishes, didn't appeal to me. Instead, my mind felt clearer, my breath felt deeper, and I simply wanted silence and simplicity.

But often, due to my schedule or social situations, I would end up eating anyway. And every time I did, something strange would happen—I would feel drained, emotionally low, and physically uneasy. The rest of the day would feel off-balance, as if I had gone against the natural rhythm of my body.

At first, I thought these were random experiences. But as they repeated, a part of me became curious. I started writing down the dates on which I felt this way. After several months, I looked back and noticed a pattern. Almost all of these days aligned with a very specific rhythm—the *Ekadashi* days in the Hindu lunar calendar.

This realization shocked me. How could my body know something my conscious mind had not yet understood? I wasn't following the calendar intentionally, yet my body was moving in sync with it.

That's when I began to study Ekadashi—not just as a religious observance, but as a deeply intelligent rhythm of nature. I learned that ancient yogis and sages had observed the same phenomena thousands of years ago. They recognized that the eleventh day after a full moon or a new moon had a unique energy—one that supported fasting, introspection, and spiritual clarity. It wasn't just about abstaining from food; it was about aligning with a deeper flow.

Since that realization, I've never looked at Ekadashi the same way. It is no longer just a date on a calendar. It has become a sacred invitation—a kind of inner festival. Twice every month, I now celebrate these days with joy and reverence. I fast not out of obligation, but out of harmony. I meditate more deeply, chant with more heart, and feel a subtle joy in honoring this ancient wisdom that my body somehow already knew.

This book is born from that personal transformation. It is my humble offering to everyone who seeks to understand the deeper meaning behind Ekadashi—not just as a tradition, but as a doorway to inner peace, natural healing, and spiritual awakening.

🏵 Why is Ekadashi Special?

- The mind becomes naturally quieter.
- Digestive demands are lowered, freeing energy for inner work.
- Spiritual practices such as japa, dhyana, and svadhyaya (study) yield exponential fruits.
- Negative karmic impressions (samskaras) are more easily purified.

🌿 Scriptural Reference:

In the *Padma Purana*, it is declared that observing Ekadashi washes away sins accumulated over many lifetimes, just as the Goddess Mother Ganga (Sacred Indian River) cleanses all impurities.

Chapter 2 — The Sacred Art of Fasting: Science, Spirit, and Discipline 🌿

A Journey into the Transformative Power of Ancient Restraint and Inner Renewal

---

🌼 The Inner Meaning of Vrata

In Sanskrit, the word Vrata (व्रत) is not merely "fasting."
It comes from the root 'vrn', meaning a sacred vow, a firm resolve.
Thus, Ekadashi Vrat is a conscious alignment — a deliberate tuning of body, mind, and spirit with the higher frequencies of Dharma.
Vrata is an invitation to stillness.
It reminds us:
"You are not the body, not the mind — you are the immortal soul shining through them."
Thus, to fast is not to punish the body — but to liberate the soul from bondage, if even for a day.

🏵 The Dual Path: Fasting and Feasting

Vedic wisdom never advocated mindless

asceticism.
Instead, it revealed a subtle dance:
• Withdraw (Upavasa) from food, from senses, from attachments.
• Feast (Mahotsava) on japa, dhyana, kirtan, seva.
Thus, Ekadashi becomes a day of inner feasting, even as the outer body is rested.
◆ Upavasa literally means "sitting near" — near what?
Near the Divine Presence within.

A Personal Approach to Observing Ekadashi

Ekadashi is not just about dietary restraint—it is a sacred invitation to align our body, mind, and soul with divine rhythms. Here is a traditional yet heartfelt way to prepare and observe Ekadashi, especially for spiritual seekers.

Preparation: On Dashami (10th Tithi)

The day before Ekadashi, known as Dashami, is crucial for purifying the body and mind in preparation.

- Sattvic Meal Before Sunset: Eat a light, clean meal before sunset. Choose fruits, warm milk, or simple boiled vegetables—avoiding onion, garlic, lentils, or grains. This helps ease digestion and promote inner calm.

- Mental Purity: Vow to abstain from arguments, anger, gossip, indulgence, violence, and distractions.
- Celibacy (Brahmacharya): Maintain physical and mental celibacy. This preserves vital life force (ojas), enhances concentration, and prepares the mind for deep prayer and reflection.
- Digital & Sensory Cleanse: Begin disconnecting from media, noise, and unnecessary speech. Limit talking and observe mindfulness in actions and words.

🕉 Sacred Vow (Sankalpa)

In the early hours of Ekadashi, just after waking and before beginning any activities, sit quietly, light a lamp, and take a personal vow:

"On this Ekadashi, I seek only the remembrance of the Lord, the service of beings, and the blossoming of my soul into Light. I dedicate this day to truthfulness, compassion, celibacy, silence, and self-restraint."

🌙 On Ekadashi Day (11th Tithi)

- Oral Hygiene without Artificial Products: Avoid modern toothpaste. Instead, chew neem or mango leaves or rinse the mouth with water or herbal decoctions.
- Avoid Violence to Nature: Do not pluck leaves or flowers from trees. If Tulsi leaves are needed, use those that have already fallen.
- Spiritual Routine:
    - After bathing, visit a temple or a quiet place of worship.
    - Listen to or recite sacred texts like the *Bhagavad Gita* or *Vishnu Sahasranama.*
    - Meditate on Lord Vishnu or your personal deity.
- Avoid Negative Company: Refrain from speaking to those engaged in slander, dishonesty, or harmful behavior. If a slip occurs, seek forgiveness through prayer and reflection.
- Silence and Mantra Japa: Practice silence (mauna), engage in chanting (especially "Om Namo Bhagavate

Vasudevaya" or the specific mantra given by your Guru), and maintain spiritual mindfulness throughout the day.

- Dietary Discipline: Avoid salt, grains, pulses, fried or processed food, carbonated drinks, or anything artificial. Consume fruits, homemade fruit juice, or small amounts of milk or water. There are other different ways devotees can observe the Ekadashi fast, depending on their health, age, and inner strength:

Type of Fast	Description
Nirjala Vrata (निर्जल व्रत)	Complete fasting without water and food for 24 hours. Ideal for strong seekers.
Phalahari Vrata (फलाहारी व्रत)	Consuming only fruits, milk, and water. Commonly observed by householders.
Sajala Vrata (सजल व्रत)	Fasting with only water intake, no solid food.

Type of Fast	Description
Ekabhukti Vrata (एकभुक्ति व्रत)	Eating only once a day, simple sattvic food without grains or beans.

- Charity and Compassion: Offer fruits or food to cows, birds, or those in need. Avoid hoarding or receiving food; instead, offer what you can.

✨ Night Vigil (Jagaran)

If possible, remain awake chanting kirtan or reading scriptures. This amplifies the spiritual power of the vrat and keeps the mind in a prayerful state. Even a few hours of wakeful devotion transforms the subtle body.

🏵 Breaking the Fast (Parana) on Dwadashi (12th Tithi)

After sunrise, but before the third muhurta (approximately within 4–6 hours), the fast is gently broken.

Traditional Practices for Breaking the Fast:

• Begin by preparing 7 dry-roasted black chickpeas (Kala Chana). These chickpeas represent purity and spiritual cleansing.
• Break each chickpea in half, so you now have 14 small pieces. This symbolizes purification and the shedding of past negativities.
• Hold the 14 pieces of broken chickpeas in your hand, and then throw them behind your head, over your shoulder. This action signifies a symbolic release of past mistakes, sins, or accumulated negative energy over the course of your life. It represents spiritual cleansing.
• After throwing the chickpeas behind you, drink 7 sips of water slowly and mindfully. The water can be plain or, if you prefer, it can be from a sacred source. This is a form of physical purification and aligns with your intention to cleanse your body and mind.
• Once you've drunk the water, you may then consume the 7 roasted chickpeas. This is a gentle way to adjust your digestive system after the fast. If you're not consuming chickpeas, you may substitute with light fruit or a small glass of milk.
• Before eating, mentally offer the food to Vishnu or your deity of choice. Recite a simple prayer of gratitude for the nourishment,

acknowledging the sacredness of the food.

• If possible, place a Tulsi leaf 🌿 on the food as an offering (leaves plucked earlier to Ekadashi). This acts as a symbol of purity and devotion, connecting your actions to a higher spiritual intention.

• Eat light prasad, like fruits, and other Sattvik foods as explained in ancient texts like *Padma Purana*.

🌿 Sattvik Food (Pure, Balanced, and Nourishing):

What is Sattvik food? Sattvik food is the essence of simplicity and nourishment. It's about choosing fresh, wholesome, and vegetarian ingredients that help balance your body, mind, and spirit. This kind of food is believed to promote clarity, mental calmness, and spiritual growth. It's not about indulgence but rather mindful eating that boosts your well-being.

Examples of Sattvik Foods:

• Fruits: Think fresh, natural fruits like apples, bananas, coconuts, and berries. These are rich in vitamins and antioxidants, perfect for a clean, energy-filled day.

• Vegetables: Leafy greens like spinach, kale,

and lettuce, alongside simple veggies like carrots and cucumbers. Light and easy to digest.

- Grains: Healthy grains such as rice, wheat, oats, and barley provide long-lasting energy.
- Nuts & Seeds: Almonds, cashews, sunflower seeds, and sesame seeds – these are nourishing and high in healthy fats.
- Dairy: Fresh milk (preferably unprocessed) and ghee (clarified butter) add purity and warmth to your meals.
- Legumes: Lentils (dal), moong dal (green gram), chickpeas (kala chana), and kidney beans offer plant-based protein and nourishment.
- Herbs & Spices: Fresh and fragrant, herbs like tulsi (holy basil), ginger, turmeric, and coriander have healing qualities.
- Simple Dishes: Traditional recipes like khichdi (a rice and lentil dish), sabzi (vegetable curry), or dal (lentils) prepared without onions or garlic.

Why Choose Sattvik? These foods are pure and light, easily digestible, and free of excessive spices. They support mental clarity, reduce stress, and help you feel connected to a sense of calm and purpose. Eating sattvik food promotes a balanced lifestyle and enhances your spiritual awareness.

🌿 Tulsi: The Sacred Companion of Ekadashi Seekers

In India, Ocimum Tenuiflorum – commonly known as Tulsi or Holy Basil – holds a uniquely sacred place, especially among those who observe Ekadashi Vrata. Though native to tropical and subtropical Asia, Tulsi's deepest roots are found in the Indian spiritual and cultural landscape, where she is revered not merely as a plant, but as a living goddess – Tulsi Devi.

Tulsi is intricately linked to Lord Vishnu and Sri Krishna, the divine forms most honored on Ekadashi. In Vaishnava homes across India, her presence is considered essential. Worship rituals often include offering a Tulsi leaf at the feet of the Lord, an act described in the *Padma Purana* as supremely meritorious.

Beyond her spiritual symbolism, Tulsi is also cultivated in Indian households for Ayurvedic and ritual purposes. She is believed to purify not just the air, but also the mind and energy field of the devotee. Many families grow Tulsi in a central courtyard or in a dedicated altar space, often surrounded by sacred markings (*rangoli, kolam*), especially maintained with devotion during Ekadashi.

Why Tulsi Matters on Ekadashi in India:

- Spiritual Participation: On Ekadashi, it is said that Tulsi too observes a fast. Out of reverence, devotees in India traditionally refrain from watering the plant or plucking its leaves on this day. This is because Tulsi is believed to fast in harmony with the devotee, and by abstaining from plucking the leaves, one shows respect for the plant's sacred vow of fasting.
- Puja Offering: A single Tulsi leaf offered on Ekadashi is believed to carry the weight of countless offerings when made with sincerity and devotion.
- Presence in Rituals: Tulsi is often placed on *Naivedyam* (offered food), in sacred water (*Charanamrita*), and on altars during Ekadashi Jagran (night vigil), amplifying the sattvic vibrations of the space.
- Cultural Continuity: From the temples of Vrindavan to the households of Tamil Nadu, Tulsi is integral to daily *puja* and

especially emphasized during the Ekadashi observance.

✿ When Not to Pluck Tulsi Leaves

While Tulsi is worshipped and revered daily, there are specific times when her leaves should not be plucked, in alignment with sacred observances:

- On Ekadashi: As mentioned, Tulsi is believed to fast on Ekadashi, and therefore, plucking her leaves on this day is avoided. This is to show respect for the fast she observes, as her spiritual energy is considered at its peak during this time.
- On Chandra Grahan (Lunar Eclipse): It is said that Tulsi, like other plants, is particularly sensitive during eclipses. During this time, her leaves should not be plucked, as the eclipse's influence may affect her spiritual potency.
- On Sundays: Sundays are traditionally seen as the day of Lord Surya (the Sun God), and some traditions recommend not plucking Tulsi leaves on this day, as the energy of the Sun is thought to be too intense for Tulsi's delicate nature.

Tulsi's Role on Ekadashi

Thus, for the Indian Ekadashi seeker, Tulsi is not only a symbol of purity and devotion but a divine ally – silently standing beside the fasting practitioner, sanctifying the vow, the offering, and the inner transformation.

Shloka on the Power of Vrata

Sanskrit:

"यानी काणि च पापानि

जन्मान्तरकृतानि च

तानी तानी विनश्यन्ति

प्रदक्षिण पदे पडे।"

Transliteration:

"Yāni kāni ca pāpāni
Janmaantara-kritāni ca
Tāni tāni vinashyanti
Pradakshiṇa pade pade"

Meaning:

"All sins accumulated over countless lifetimes are dissolved by each step taken in sacred observances like Ekadashi."

Chapter 3 — Understanding The Divine Mathematics of Time 🌿

Exploring the Sacred Calendar of Sanatana Dharma and the Cosmic Rhythm of Days

---

🏵 Introduction: Cosmic Time-Keeping

In the Vedic tradition, time is not measured merely by mechanical clocks, but by the rhythms of the cosmos — the moon's waxing and waning, the sun's journeys across the zodiac, and the delicate dance of celestial forces.

Tithi is one of the most sacred and scientific measures of this flow.

Unlike the Western calendar which fixes months by solar calculation, the Hindu calendar (Panchanga) integrates both the lunar and solar movements, creating a dynamic, living map of Time that resonates with human consciousness.

🏵 What is a Tithi?

◇ Definition:

Tithi (तिथि) is the lunar day — the time it takes for the angular distance between the sun and the moon to increase by 12°.

🏵 Mathematical Beauty of Tithi

Suppose:

1. Moon moves ~12° relative to Sun each day.
2. A lunar cycle = about 29.5 solar days.

Thus,
30 Tithis × ~0.95 = ~29.5 days.

◆ This is why the Hindu lunar month nearly matches one Moon cycle (New Moon to New Moon), but slight differences occur — leading to occasional adjustments like Adhik Maas (extra month).

✿ The 15 Tithis of Each Paksha

The lunar month is divided into two halves (Pakshas). Each Paksha consists of the following 15 Tithis:

- Pratipada (1st)
- Dwitiya (2nd)
- Tritiya (3rd)
- Chaturthi (4th)
- Panchami (5th)
- Shashthi (6th)
- Saptami (7th)
- Ashtami (8th)
- Navami (9th)
- Dashami (10th)
- **Ekadashi (11th)**
- Dwadashi (12th)
- Trayodashi (13th)
- Chaturdashi (14th)
- Purnima (Full Moon) or Amavasya (New Moon)

Ekadashi always falls on the 11th Tithi — either in the waxing (Shukla) or waning (Krishna) phase.

Phase	Name	Meaning
Shukla Paksha	Bright half	Waxing moon (New Moon to Full Moon)

Phase	Name	Meaning
Krishna Paksha	Dark half	Waning moon (Full Moon to New Moon)

🏵 Hindu Months (Māsa) and Their Approximate Gregorian Timing

Sanskrit Name	Hindi Name	Gregorian Month (Approx)
Chaitra	चैत्र	March–April
Vaishakha	वैशाख	April–May
Jyeshtha	ज्येष्ठ	May–June
Ashadha	आषाढ़	June–July
Shravana	श्रावण	July–August
Bhadrapada	भाद्रपद	August–September
Ashwin	आश्विन	September–October
Kartika	कार्तिक	October–November
Margashirsha	मार्गशीर्ष	November–December

Sanskrit Name	Hindi Name	Gregorian Month (Approx)
Pausha	पौष	December–January
Magha	माघ	January–February
Phalguna	फाल्गुन	February–March

These months may shift slightly based on lunar motion and regional traditions.

🏵 Special Note: Adhik Maas (The Extra Month)

Approximately every 2.5 to 3 years, the lunar calendar falls behind the solar calendar.
To realign, an extra month called Adhik Maas is inserted.

🌷 During this month:

- No weddings or major ceremonies are performed.
- It is considered highly auspicious for spiritual practices, pilgrimages, donations, and Ekadashi observances.

Even in modern solar calendars, Leap Years are added every 4 years to balance Earth's revolution and calendar counting.

Nakshatras: The Cosmic Constellations

In Hindu astrology, the Moon's journey is mapped through 27 Nakshatras or lunar constellations. These Nakshatras represent different zones or sections along the Moon's orbit, each of which governs specific energies, traits, and tendencies. The Moon, the emotional and mental planet in astrology, moves through one Nakshatra approximately every day, guiding the emotional flow of individuals born under its influence.

- How It Connects to Us: Each Nakshatra is associated with a unique energy and deity, which influences daily activities, choices, and spiritual practices. These lunar constellations are considered more than just astronomical points; they represent the interface between the earthly and divine, linking human life to celestial bodies.

Yoga: The Sun-Moon Dance

In Hindu timekeeping, Yoga refers to the special combination of the Sun and Moon's positions. There are 27 different Yogas, each providing a unique celestial influence. The term "Yoga" in this context is a cosmic union, symbolizing the fusion of masculine and feminine energies—the Sun and the Moon.

- How It Connects to Us: The Sun represents the masculine energy (consciousness, action, power), while the Moon represents feminine energy (intuition, receptivity, emotion). The balance between these energies is essential for spiritual growth, and the positioning of these two celestial bodies can dictate favorable or unfavorable times for specific activities.

Karana: Dividing the Tithi

Karana divides each Tithi (the lunar day) into two halves. A Tithi is the time it takes for the Moon to travel 12 degrees along the ecliptic. A full moon or new moon is the culmination of the 15-day cycle, and each Tithi represents a specific segment of the Moon's journey. There are 11 different Karanas, and each one affects the nature of the day.

- How It Connects to Us: The first half of the Tithi is said to be more active and appropriate for new beginnings, while the second half is ideal for reflection and completion. The choice of Karana determines auspiciousness for ceremonies, rituals, or even personal endeavors, aligning your activities with the rhythm of the cosmos.

The Panchang is an essential tool for daily life in Hindu tradition. It's not just a calendar but a guide that aligns an individual's routine with the natural flow of time, ensuring harmony with the Universe. The Panchang includes:

- Tithi: The lunar day, an important marker for the auspiciousness of activities.
- Nakshatra: The constellation the Moon is in, influencing moods, actions, and intentions.
- Yoga: The cosmic dance between the Sun and Moon, guiding ideal moments for spiritual practices.
- Karana: The specific division of the Tithi, providing insight into when to act and when to rest.
- Vara: Each day of the week (Vara) is associated with a specific planet and its deity: Sunday with the Sun (Surya), Monday with the Moon (Chandra), Tuesday with Mars (Mangala), Wednesday with Mercury (Budh), Thursday with Jupiter (Brihaspati),

Friday with Venus (Shukra), and Saturday with Saturn (Shani), each influencing the energies and activities of the day.

🏵 How to Know When to Fast (Especially on Ekadashi)

☞ Always check the Panchang (the traditional Hindu calendar).

☞ If Ekadashi Tithi begins before sunrise, you fast on that day.

If it begins after sunrise, then fast the next day.

🌿 Example:

- If Ekadashi starts at 5 AM → Fast that day.
- If Ekadashi starts at 10 AM → Fast the next day.

This rule helps in following the cosmic rhythm properly.

A Personal Approach to Observing Ekadashi

In many traditional practices, Ekadashi, the sacred day of fasting and devotion to Lord Vishnu, is observed based on the specific timing of the Ekadashi Tithi (lunar day) in the Hindu calendar. Typically, Ekadashi begins at the start of the Ekadashi Tithi and ends when the following day's Tithi, Dwadashi, begins. To get the most accurate timing for Ekadashi, you can use online tools like Panchang or Hindu calendar apps.

However, depending on the timing of the Tithi—especially when the Ekadashi Tithi ends after sunrise—many devotees, like myself, may choose to observe Ekadashi on the previous day. For example, if the Ekadashi Tithi ends just one hour after sunrise, I personally choose to celebrate it on the day before, when the Tithi is predominantly active. This allows me to align my observance with the main part of the day and ensures that I'm fasting and practicing devotion during the most spiritually significant part of the Tithi.

This approach is based on my understanding and spiritual intuition. For me, it's not just about following the precise timing of the Tithi but about creating a meaningful connection with the divine on this sacred day. By doing this, I feel that my devotion and efforts are more focused, as I am honoring Ekadashi in a way that resonates deeply with my heart.

In essence, Ekadashi is a deeply personal and spiritual practice, and different devotees may choose to observe it in ways that align with their individual understanding and connection with their Deity. While traditional observances focus on the exact timing of the Tithi with sunrise method, the most important aspect is the devotion and purity with which the fast is observed.

Shloka on the Glory of Tithis

Sanskrit:

"तिथिर्वैभवमाख्यां येन जन्मशतैरपि।

न लभ्यते नरैर्मर्त्यैः स लभ्यते व्रतैरपि॥"

Transliteration:

"Tithirvaibhavamākhyaami
Yena janma-shatairapi
Na labhyate narairmartyaih
Sa labhyate vratairapi"

Meaning:

"The glory attained by observing sacred Tithis cannot be attained even through hundreds of human births."

Chapter 4 — The Sacred Science Behind Fasting 🌿

A Divine Alchemy of Body, Mind, and Spirit

🌿 The Ancient Art of Fasting

In the ageless wisdom of Sanātana Dharma, fasting (*Upavāsa*, उपवास) is not seen as starvation, but as moving closer to the Divine — "*Upa*" = *near*, "*Vāsa*" = *to dwell.*

Thus, to fast is to dwell near God, to empty the body and mind of noise, and to invite the sacred breath of clarity and grace

Ekadashi fasting stands at the heart of this tradition.
It is an energetic cleansing — a day when human consciousness can ascend swiftly towards its luminous Source.

The *Mahabharata* proclaims:

"Fasting is the ladder to heaven; the purifier of the body and mind"

Spiritual Purpose: Purification and Expansion

Yet, fasting is far more than a bodily process. It is a sacred tapasya (inner fire), a means to:

- Burn karmic impressions (samskaras).
- Awaken dormant energies (kundalini).
- Expand awareness beyond physical cravings.

Thus, Ekadashi fasting gently trains the seeker's mind away from compulsive habits, and reorients it toward divine longing.

The Energetics of Food and Ekadashi

According to Ayurveda, different foods carry different gunas (qualities):

- Grains and legumes are heavy (tamasic).
- Fresh fruits, nuts, and dairy are light and sattvic.

On Ekadashi, abstaining from heavy foods allows the prana (life energy) to move freely, aiding meditation and higher states of consciousness.

Hence, on Ekadashi:

- Grains, lentils, beans, and certain vegetables (like onions, garlic) are avoided.
- Fruits, roots (like sweet potatoes), milk, and water are embraced.

Scientific Note: Grains and legumes ferment heavily during digestion, burdening the system. Their temporary avoidance eases the body's inner purification.

✿ Emotional Detoxification

Fasting on Ekadashi also promotes emotional purification.
When digestion rests, emotional toxins — suppressed fears, anger, sadness — surface naturally.

This is why Ekadashi observances emphasize:

- Silence (Mauna)
- Mantra chanting
- Prayer and kirtan
- Seva (selfless service)

Thus, fasting becomes not a suppression, but a celebration of the inner light emerging from within.

How to Fast Gracefully

The scriptures lovingly guide us in fasting without violence to the body:

Thus:

- Elderly, children, sick, and pregnant women are allowed mild fasts (phalahar — fruits and milk).
- The bhava (intention) matters more than the strictness.

Compassion to oneself is considered dharmic.

Chapter 5 — Utpanna Ekadashi: The Birth of Divine Goddess 🌿

🌸 The Day of Sacred Beginnings — Utpanna Ekadashi

- **English Name**: Utpanna Ekadashi
- **Hindi Name**: उत्पन्ना एकादशी
- **Pronunciation**: Utpannā Ekādaśī

📅 Tithi and Timing

• **Hindu Calendar Tithi**: Kārtika Krishna Paksha Ekadashi (कार्तिक कृष्ण पक्ष एकादशी)

• **Approximate Gregorian Timing**: November–December

🌙 Astronomical Note:

This Ekadashi occurs during the waning phase of the moon, a time when nature itself turns inward. Fasting during this phase aligns the body's detox rhythms and supports spiritual awakening.

🏵 Significance of Utpanna Ekadashi

Utpanna Ekadashi marks a cosmic beginning

— the first appearance of Ekadashi Devi (Goddess), the divine personification of the eleventh lunar day.

This day is seen as the birth of the protective spiritual energy that aids devotees in overcoming negativity, desires, and cycles of karma.

According to the *Padma Purana*, by observing Utpanna Ekadashi, devotees not only receive the merit of all other Ekadashis combined but also gain the strength to embark upon a lifetime of higher living.

It is said:

"Those who observe this Ekadashi are eternally protected by the compassionate power of Ekadashi Devi."

🛕 The Story of Utpanna Ekadashi: Triumph Over the Demon Mura

Yudhishthir is a central character in the Indian epic, the *Mahabharata*. He is one of the five Pandavas, the sons of King Pandu and his queens Kunti and Madri. Yudhishthir is known for his wisdom, righteousness, and unwavering commitment to truth and dharma (righteous duty).

The story begins with Yudhishthir, the eldest of the Pandavas, asking Lord Krishna, "O Lord, how did the auspicious Ekadashi Tithi come into existence? Why is it considered so sacred, and how did the gods receive it?"

Lord Krishna, with a knowing smile, replied: "Yudhishthir, the story goes back to ancient times, during the Satya Yuga. There lived a powerful demon named Mura, whose strength and terror were beyond measure. His very presence sent shockwaves through the heavens, and he defeated all the gods, casting them out of their heavenly realm. The gods, defeated and helpless, wandered on Earth, disheartened and looking for refuge."

This was a time of great mysticism. The laws of nature and the balance of the universe seemed to hang by a thread. It was a world where divine forces and powerful beings could alter the course of destiny with a single word or action.

One day, the gods, desperate for salvation, went to Lord Shiva, the supreme god, to plead for help. They said, "O Mahadev Shiva, we have been driven out of the heavens by Mura, and we wander like lost souls on Earth. We cannot remain in the mortal world, for it brings us no peace. What should we do? To whom should we turn for protection?"

Lord Shiva, in his infinite wisdom, gazed at the troubled gods and said: "You must go to Lord Vishnu, the one who protects all beings and whose divine power holds the fabric of the universe together. It is he who will offer you refuge."

The gods, in deep faith and reverence, set out for the Ksheer Sagar (Ocean of Milk), where Lord Vishnu rested on his divine serpent, Shesha Naag. As they reached him, they offered their humble prayers, knowing that they were in the presence of a being whose power was beyond mortal comprehension. There was an undeniable mystical energy in the surroundings as they approached the Lord, whose very presence seemed to radiate the essence of the universe.

The gods bowed down and said: "O Lord of Lords, we seek your shelter. You are the father of all, the mother, the cause of everything. You are the protector of both the gods and the demons. It is You who guides the very forces of nature. Please, O Lord, protect us from Mura, the demon who has cast us out of the heavens."

Lord Vishnu, ever compassionate, listened intently and asked, "What is this demon Mura like? Where does he reside, and what are his powers?"

The gods, with deep reverence, replied, "O Lord, this demon is born from the lineage of Talajangha, a fearsome asura. His name, Mura, is known far and wide for his strength. He resides in the city of Chandravati and has cast us from the heavens. He controls all the divine forces, replacing the gods with his own creations. O Lord, we cannot defeat him on our own."

As the gods explained the situation, a sense of mysticism hung in the air. The very forces of creation seemed to be at the mercy of a demon, which posed an enigma. How could such a being, born of darkness, overpower the cosmic balance that Vishnu maintained?

Lord Vishnu, perceiving the greater mystery behind these events, took the gods with him to the city of Chandravati. As they entered, Vishnu saw Mura, the demon, standing victorious, bellowing in triumph as the gods scattered in fear. The demon, seeing Lord Vishnu, shouted, "Stand still, O Lord! You cannot escape me!"

In that moment, the divine energy around Vishnu grew intense. With a simple, yet powerful gesture, Lord Vishnu began to strike down Mura's forces. His divine arrows, infused with the very power of creation, pierced the demon's army, sending shockwaves through the air. The mystical power of Vishnu was so great that even the earth trembled at his actions.

But the battle didn't end there. As the dust settled, Vishnu proceeded to the cave of Singhavati in Badrikaashram, a mystical place that was twelve yojanas long (about 156 kilometers or 97 miles). Within this cave, only one door existed, as if it were designed for the meeting of divinity and darkness. Vishnu entered, and as he lay down to rest, the mysterious force of the universe seemed to pause, waiting for what would come next.

Mura, in his hatred, followed Lord Vishnu into the cave. As he entered, he saw Vishnu resting peacefully, and an evil thought took root in his heart. "This is the god who has defeated my army," Mura thought. "Now, I will strike him down while he sleeps."

At that moment, an extraordinary event occurred. From Lord Vishnu's body emerged a divine and radiant goddess, whose beauty and presence could not be described in mere mortal terms. She was an embodiment of divine power and mystery, her form the perfect blend of elegance and strength. She exuded an ethereal glow, and her very presence seemed to command the elements of the universe.

As she rose from Lord Vishnu's being, a divine aura filled the cave. The very air shimmered with her energy, and the demon Mura, upon seeing her, was overwhelmed with awe and fear. Her beauty was so captivating, yet her power was terrifying.

In that strange, quiet moment, the goddess Ekadashi let out a cold, haunting roar that shook the edges of reality. The power she released couldn't be measured or understood. The demon king Mura, once feared for his immense strength, crumbled in an instant. His body and soul split apart, turned to ash. Some whisper that the hidden realms still echo with that roar.

As Mura's body lay in ruin, Lord Vishnu awoke and saw the demon defeated. He turned to the radiant goddess and asked, "Who has slain this demon? This being was a great threat, and now he is gone. Tell me, who is the one who has brought this victory?"

The goddess, with a serene smile, answered, "O Lord, by Your grace, I have destroyed this great demon."

Vishnu, recognizing the mystery, and the power of this divine being, smiled and said,

"O blessed one, you have freed the worlds from this great evil. Ask for any boon you wish, for you are a rare and divine being. I shall grant it, for your actions have restored balance in the universe."

The goddess, with her captivating presence and profound wisdom, replied, "O Lord, if You are pleased, I wish to be known as Ekadashi, the goddess who dispels all sins and grants blessings to those who observe my fast. May all who fast on this day receive the greatest rewards of prosperity, peace, and liberation."

Lord Vishnu, deeply moved by her words, said:

"*O radiant one! Because you have arisen on the eleventh day and protected all creation, you shall be known as 'Ekadashi.' Those who honor you shall attain liberation and my eternal abode.*"

Thus, Ekadashi became a mystical and sacred day, with a power that transcends time and space. It is a day when divine energy flows freely, and those who observe it with devotion are said to receive liberation from all sins. The mystery of Ekadashi lies in its divine origin and the cosmic power it holds, which can cleanse the soul and restore balance to the universe.

Lord Krishna concludes: "Yudhishthir, Ekadashi is not just a day of fasting; it is a cosmic force, an energy that purifies the soul and brings balance to the world. Whether observed in the waxing or waning phase, it holds the power to cleanse all sins and grant divine blessings. The observance of Ekadashi is a doorway to liberation, where the mysteries of the universe are unveiled for those who seek the truth."

ॐ Meditation

On this sacred day, sit silently after mantra chanting.
Focus on the point between your eyebrows (Ajna chakra) while gently breathing in and out.
Visualize Lord Vishnu, sleeping peacefully on the cosmic ocean, surrounded by lotuses of light.
Let the mantra "*Aum Vishnave Namah*" vibrate in your heart.

✿ Mantra

Sanskrit:

शान्ताकारं भुजगशयनं पद्मनाभं सुरेशम्।
विश्वाधारं गगनसदृशं मेघवर्णं शुभाङ्गम्॥

Transliteration:

Śāntākāraṁ bhujagaśayanaṁ padmanābhaṁ sureśam,
Viśvādhāraṁ gaganasadṛśaṁ meghavarṇaṁ śubhāṅgam.

Meaning:

"I bow to Lord Vishnu, whose form is tranquil, who reclines upon the serpent, whose navel births the lotus, Lord of all gods, supporter of the universe, boundless like the sky."

Chapter 6 — Mokshada Ekadashi: The Deliverer of Liberation 🌿

🌷 The Day of Ultimate Freedom — Mokshada Ekadashi

- **English Name:** Mokshada Ekadashi
- **Hindi Name:** मोक्षदा एकादशी
- **Pronunciation:** Mokṣadā Ekādaśī

📅 Tithi and Timing

- **Hindu Calendar Tithi:** Mārgaśīrṣa Shukla Paksha Ekadashi (मार्गशीर्ष शुक्ल पक्ष एकादशी)
- **Approximate Gregorian Calendar Timing:** November–December

🌙 Astronomical Note:

As the waxing moon strengthens during Shukla Paksha, Mokshada Ekadashi provides heightened spiritual energy, aiding efforts to transcend karmic bondage

The Story of Mokshada Ekadashi

In the serene month of Margashirsha (a sacred month in the Hindu lunar calendar), as the moon grew fuller during the Shukla Paksha (waxing moon phase), King Yudhishthira—the eldest Pandava, wise and devoted—approached Lord Krishna, his divine guide and friend.

He asked with deep reverence:

"O Lord of the Universe, please tell me what Ekadashi (11th lunar day sacred for fasting and worship) falls in this month. What are its rituals, and which deity is worshipped on this holy day?"

Smiling with divine grace, Lord Krishna replied:

"O noble King, the Ekadashi that falls during the Shukla Paksha of Margashirsha is known as Mokshada Ekadashi (Ekadashi that grants liberation from the cycle of birth and death). Simply hearing about its glory is equal to performing the Vajpayee Yajna (a grand Vedic fire ritual that grants great spiritual merit). On this sacred day, devotees must worship Lord Damodara (a loving form of Krishna as a child tied with a rope by his mother) with Tulsi leaves (holy basil symbolizing purity) and fragrant incense. Lighting lamps and offering heartfelt prayers is essential. One must observe fasting with sincerity, starting from the previous day (Dashami)."

"On this night, devotees should stay awake singing, dancing, and praising the Lord. Those who offer the merit of this day to their ancestors (departed forefathers) can release them from lower realms and grant them salvation. There is no doubt in the power of this observance."

Lord Krishna proceeds to tell the story:

Long ago, in the divine and fragrant land of Champak Nagar, ruled a noble king named Vaikhanas. Deeply religious and righteous, he lived a life devoted to dharma (righteousness).

One night, as the stars shimmered with an unnatural stillness and the wind whispered secrets, King Vaikhanas was seized by a dream darker than night itself.

He stood in a barren, cold world—a land of twisted trees, charred soil, and skies of burning ash. From the fog emerged wailing voices, filled with agony. The air grew thick with the smell of decay. Chains clanked in the distance. And then—he saw them.

His ancestors.

Their forms were shadowed, pale, and trembling—trapped in pits of sorrow, surrounded by flames that did not burn but tormented the soul. Their eyes, hollow with centuries of grief, met his.

They cried:

"Son... hear us! We are your blood! Cursed by past sins, we dwell in this hellish realm. You alone can free us! You, our flesh and blood—bring us light!"

Their hands reached out, but the darkness dragged them down again. Their cries echoed endlessly, until Vaikhanas jolted awake, soaked in sweat and horror-stricken.

Troubled beyond words, the king rushed at dawn to consult the brahmins (Hindu priests). He said:

"I have seen my forefathers in torment. I cannot bear their suffering. What penance, what ritual, can free them from such a fate?"

The sages answered:

"O King, nearby lives the great sage Parvat (a wise seer and knower of time and truth). He alone can guide you."

Without delay, Vaikhanas ventured into the sacred mountains, journeying through thick forests and mist-covered paths. Finally, he reached the ashram (hermitage) of Sage Parvat, and bowed deeply at his feet.

The sage, seeing the king's anguish, meditated silently. Then he opened his eyes and spoke:

"O King, I have seen your truth. Salvation lies in observing Mokshada Ekadashi. On this day, fast with purity, worship Lord Damodara, and offer the merit of your worship to your ancestors. They shall be freed."

Lord Shri Krishna says:
"O Yudhishthira! Hearing the sage's words, the king returned to his palace. When the auspicious month of *Margashirsha* arrived, King Vaikhanas observed the 'Mokshada Ekadashi' fast as instructed by the sage, and offered the accrued merit to his father along with all his ancestors.

As soon as he did so, flowers began to rain down from the sky. King Vaikhanasa's father, along with the ancestors, was liberated from hell and rose into the sky. Appearing before the king, he spoke these sacred words:
'My son! May you be blessed.'

Saying this, he ascended to heaven.

O King! One who observes this auspicious *Mokshada Ekadashi* fast has all their sins destroyed and attains liberation after death. This liberating *Mokshada Ekadashi* is like a wish-fulfilling gem (*Chintamani*) for humans, granting all desires.

Simply by reading or hearing this sacred account (*mahatmya*), one receives the merit equivalent to performing a *Vajapeya* yajna (a grand Vedic sacrifice)."

ॐ Meditation

Sit silently after your evening prayer.
Visualize a radiant river of light flowing from your heart upward, dissolving into the infinite sky.
Each breath merges your little self into the vast cosmic Self.
Repeat silently:
"Aham Brahmasmi" (I am Universe: non-dual awareness where the boundary between self and cosmos dissolves).
After meditation, softly say in your mind:
"On this sacred day, I meditate for the liberation of my ancestors.
May their souls be free, and may peace flow across my lineage."
Let the words dissolve into silence. Bow inwardly in gratitude and stillness.

✿ Mantra

Sanskrit:

नमः पुण्याय पुण्याय पुण्यतीर्थाय ते नमः।
नमो धर्माय धर्माय सर्वधर्माय ते नमः॥

Transliteration:

Namaḥ puṇyāya puṇyāya puṇyatīrthāya te namaḥ,
Namo dharmāya dharmāya sarvadharmāya te namaḥ.

Meaning:

"Salutations to the Embodiment of all purity and virtue, to the sacred pilgrimage of righteousness”

Enjoying the Reading?

If *Ekadashi – The Eleventh Day* has inspired you or touched your spirit, I'd love to hear from you!

Your honest review on Amazon helps fellow readers discover this book and supports me as an independent author.

Scan the QR Code below to leave a review

—or—

Visit this link:

https://www.amazon.com/review/create-review?asin=9334287195

It only takes a minute, and your support means so much. Thank you for being part of this journey!

Chapter 7 — Safala Ekadashi: The Fruitful Triumph 🌿

🌷 The Day of Success and Prosperity — Safala Ekadashi

- **English Name**: Safala Ekadashi
- **Hindi Name**: सफला एकादशी
- **Pronunciation**: Safalā Ekādaśī

📅 Tithi and Timing

- **Hindu Calendar Tithi**: Pauṣa Krishna Paksha Ekadashi (पौष कृष्ण पक्ष एकादशी)
- **Approximate Gregorian Calendar Timing**: December–January

---

🌸 Astronomical Note

During the waning phase of the moon (Krishna Paksha), the body's detoxification processes intensify, making fasting more effective both physically and karmically. This period is considered auspicious for spiritual practices and self-purification.

✿ Significance of Safala Ekadashi

Safala Ekadashi is celebrated as the day when sincere efforts, prayers, and austerities blossom into tangible success. The word "Safala" itself means "Fruitful" or "Successful." It is said that those who observe this Ekadashi with devotion are blessed with prosperity, success in endeavors, and liberation from failures. The Skanda Purana declares:

"The merits obtained by observing Safala Ekadashi outweigh those gained by performing a thousand Ashvamedha Yajna ".

Thus, it is a powerful day for invoking divine grace upon material and spiritual pursuits.

The Story of Safala Ekadashi: The Redemption of Lumbhaka

Once, King Yudhishthira, the wise ruler, asked Lord Krishna, "O Lord, tell me the name of the Ekadashi that falls during the Krishna Paksha (dark fortnight) of the month of Pausha (which corresponds to the month of Margashirsha in

Maharashtra and Gujarat), its significance, its rituals, and the deity worshipped on that day."

Lord Krishna replied with reverence, "O King! Even grand yajnas (rituals) and sacrifices, which are performed with immense devotion and wealth, do not please me as much as the observance of Ekadashi. The Ekadashi that occurs during the Krishna Paksha in Pausha is known as *Saphala Ekadashi* (the fruitful or successful Ekadashi). On this sacred day, the worship of Lord Narayana (Vishnu) must be done with great devotion and sincerity. Among the many auspicious days, Ekadashi stands as supreme, just as among serpents, Sheshanaga (the divine serpent) is revered, among birds, Garuda (the mythical eagle) is worshipped, and among deities, Lord Vishnu is the most venerated."

"On *Saphala Ekadashi*, one should offer specific fruits such as coconut, betel nuts, jujube, lemons, pomegranates, and especially mangoes, to Lord Vishnu. These fruits should be offered along with incense and lamps in a well-prepared worship ritual. The unique aspect of *Saphala Ekadashi* is the offering of lamps (deep daan). On this night, devotees should stay awake in devotion, for the benefits gained from such night vigils are more significant than years of austere penance."

"Now listen, O King, to the fascinating tale associated with *Saphala Ekadashi*."

There was once a city named Champavati, which was the capital of the noble King Mahismat. King Mahismat had five sons, one of whom was named Lumbhaka. Lumbhaka, however, was notorious for his wicked deeds. He indulged in sinful activities, spending his life in debauchery and indulging in worldly pleasures. He spent the wealth of his father on sinful activities and often spoke ill of both sages and gods. His immoral behavior deeply distressed his father, King Mahismat, and hence he was given the name 'Lumbhaka', meaning one who is bent or twisted in his ways. Eventually, Lumbhaka was exiled from the kingdom by his father and brothers.

Lumbhaka wandered deep into the forest, where he began to rob the wealth of passing travelers. One night, while attempting to loot a village, he was caught by the guards. However, when he revealed his identity as the son of King Mahismat, the guards, being respectful of the royal lineage, released him. He returned to the forest and lived on the fruits of the trees and animal flesh. One such nearby place, in the depths of the forest stood a Peepal (often associated with Lord Vishnu in Hinduism) tree, ancient and gnarled, its roots twisted like serpents, grasping the earth with a grip that seemed both powerful and unnatural. The tree was massive, its canopy spreading wide like a dark shadow, blocking out the sunlight even at noon. Its leaves, large and dark, rustled in the wind, but not in a way that was soothing. There was something unsettling about the way they whispered as though the tree was alive, speaking secrets in an ancient tongue only the wind could understand. Lumbhaka started to live near it, unaware that his life was about to change.

By some divine intervention, Lumbhaka, through a series of fortunate events, unknowingly observed *Saphala Ekadashi*. On the day of the *Krishna Paksha* Ekadashi in Pausha, he ate the fruits from the trees and, due to exhaustion, spent the entire night shivering from the cold. Even as the sun rose the next morning, he had not regained his senses. He lay unconscious throughout the day, and even during *Saphala Ekadashi*, he remained oblivious to the passing hours. But by noon, he regained his awareness.

Weak and famished, Lumbhaka stumbled into the forest, desperately searching for food. He gathered as many fruits as he could carry and made his way back to the Peepal tree. There, he offered the fruits to the tree and said, "May Lord Vishnu, who resides in the form of this tree, be pleased with this humble offering." He did not sleep that night, maintaining his vigil, not realizing that he had observed the sacred *Saphala Ekadashi.*

Suddenly, a voice echoed from the heavens, "O prince, through your devotion to *Saphala Ekadashi*, you shall not only reclaim your kingdom but will also attain liberation (moksha)."

Hearing this divine proclamation, Lumbhaka accepted the blessing with gratitude. As a result, his appearance transformed, becoming radiant with divine light. He then devoted himself to the worship of Lord Vishnu, adorning himself with celestial jewels. Lumbhaka returned to his kingdom and ruled it wisely for many years.

Lumbhaka had a son named Manoj. When Manoj grew up, Lumbhaka, no longer attached to the material world, abdicated the throne in favor of his son and retired to the path of devotion, where he was blessed with eternal peace in the presence of Lord Krishna. This devotion ensured that Lumbhaka would never again experience sorrow, as he remained in the eternal realm of bliss.

"O King," concluded Lord Krishna, "the one who observes *Saphala Ekadashi* with full devotion attains both material happiness in this world and spiritual liberation (moksha) in the afterlife. By reading, hearing, or following the rituals of *Saphala Ekadashi*, a person earns the merit equivalent to performing the grand Rajasuya Yajna".

ॐ Meditation

At midnight or during deep night hours:

- Visualize yourself sitting under an immense, sacred peepal tree.
- Feel its vast roots connecting your soul to the Earth, and its soaring branches lifting your spirit toward the stars.
- With each inhalation, draw the power of purity.
- With each exhalation, release karmic burdens into the Infinite.

Repeat internally:

"Vishvam Vishnur Vashatkaraḥ"

("The Universe itself is Vishnu.")

This visualization dissolves inner negativity, aligning you with cosmic success.

🏵 Mantra

Sanskrit:

शान्ताकारं भुजगशयनं पद्मनाभं सुरेशं ।

विश्वाधारं गगनसदृशं मेघवर्णं शुभाङ्गम्॥

Transliteration:
Śāntākāraṁ Bhujagaśayanaṁ Padmanābhaṁ Sureśaṁ,
Viśvādhāraṁ Gaganasadṛśaṁ Meghavarṇaṁ Śubhāṅgam.

Meaning:

"I bow to the Serene Lord Vishnu, resting on Ananta-Shesha, whose navel blooms the lotus of creation, who is the support of the universe, vast as the sky, dark as the monsoon cloud, and radiant with auspicious beauty".

Chapter 8 — Putrada Ekadashi: The Bestower of Progeny 🌿

🌷 The Day of Fulfillment — Putrada Ekadashi

- **English Name**: Putrada Ekadashi
- **Hindi Name**: पुत्रदा एकादशी
- **Pronunciation**: *Putradā Ekādaśī*

📅 Tithi and Timing

- **Hindu Calendar Tithi**: Pauṣa Shukla Paksha Ekadashi (पौष शुक्ल पक्ष एकादशी)
- **Approximate Gregorian Calendar Timing**: January

🌷 Astronomical Note:

During the waxing phase (Shukla Paksha), the moon's energies rise, symbolizing growth and expansion. Observing a fast at this time helps plant spiritual seeds for worldly and divine fulfilment.

The Story of Putrada Ekadashi: The Mysterious Journey of King Suketuman

Yudhishthir spoke:
"O Krishna! Please kindly tell me the significance of the Ekadashi that falls during the Shukla Paksha (waxing phase) of the month of Pausha. What is its name?

Lord Krishna said:
"O King! The Ekadashi that falls during the Shukla Paksha of the month of Pausha is called 'Putrada Ekadashi'."

Long ago, in the Bhadravatipuri kingdom, there lived a wise and noble king, Suketuman, and his beloved queen, Shaivya. However, despite their love, they were childless. Year after year, they prayed to the gods for a child, but their hearts remained heavy, burdened with the absence of an heir. Even their parents, in their old age, lamented, "After the king, who will continue our lineage? Who will perform our funeral rites and carry on our legacy?"

In a moment of deep sorrow, King Suketuman decided to leave the palace and wander into the dense forest in search of solace. His decision was known only to the royal family.

Saddling his horse, he rode into the unknown wilderness, where the trees whispered ancient secrets and wild animals roamed freely. The forest was alive with sounds: jackals howled in the distance, owls hooted eerily, and the occasional roar of a bear echoed through the trees. Yet, the king felt drawn into its mystery.

As the sun reached its zenith, hunger and thirst gripped the king. Wandering in search of water, he finally stumbled upon a beautiful lake, where a group of holy sages (wise ascetics) sat, absorbed in the chanting of ancient scriptures. The sages were meditating by the lake, performing their spiritual practices, and their peaceful presence filled the air with a divine aura.

The sight of these sages filled the king's heart with awe and reverence. Dismounting from his horse, the king approached them respectfully and bowed deeply. These sages, known for their devotion to Lord Vishnu, were followers of the practice of *Upavas* (a sacred fast).

The sages, seeing the king's humility, spoke in unison:
"King Suketuman, your devotion pleases us."

The king, eager to understand the mysteries before him, asked:

"Who are you, great sages? Why have you gathered here, and what is it that you seek?"

The sages responded with wisdom:
"O King, we are Vedic sages, and we have come here to purify ourselves before the sacred month of Magha (a highly auspicious time for spiritual practices). In five days, the great river will open its gates for ritual bathing. But today, O King, is an extraordinary day—the day of Putrada Ekadashi. It is a day when those who fast and worship Lord Vishnu with devotion are blessed with children. This day is said to bestow divine blessings upon all those who observe it with a pure heart."

The king's heart raced with hope, as he saw the divine opportunity before him. He asked, "Great sages, if you are pleased with me, please grant me the blessing of a child, for this is my only desire in this world."

The sages smiled and responded:
"O King, if you observe the fast of Putrada Ekadashi, your wish will surely be fulfilled. The grace of Lord Vishnu will bless you with a son who will carry on your lineage."

Following the guidance of the sages, King Suketuman returned to his kingdom and observed the fast of Putrada Ekadashi with the utmost devotion. He offered fruits such as coconuts, pomegranates, and mangoes to Lord Vishnu and chanted his sacred names throughout the day. As night fell, the king stayed awake, praying and offering incense to Lord Vishnu, experiencing a profound sense of peace and divine presence.

After some time, the king overjoyed to discover that the queen, Shaivya, was pregnant. Soon, a blessed child was born to them, a son who would grow up to be a wise and powerful ruler, loved by all. The entire kingdom rejoiced in the divine blessings of Putrada Ekadashi, for the king's sorrow had been erased, and his family was complete.

Lord Krishna, turning to Yudhishthir, continued:
"O Yudhishthir! The fast of Putrada Ekadashi is powerful. It not only grants the boon of children but also ensures freedom from the cycle of birth and death. It is a day of immense spiritual significance. Those who observe this fast with pure devotion are blessed with peace, prosperity, and eternal joy."

Putrada Ekadashi, the Ekadashi that blesses devotees with children, is a sacred day for those seeking divine blessings.

🕉 Meditation

After midnight, seat yourself quietly, spine straight.
Visualize a luminous seed — golden and warm — planted within your heart.
With each breath, it grows roots into the earth and shoots toward the heavens.
Silently affirm:
"From the seed of devotion, springs the tree of eternal joy."
This meditation, called *Beeja Dharana* (Seed Visualization), harmonizes personal desires with cosmic will.

Mantra

Sanskrit:
ॐ श्रीं श्रीं कृष्णाय गोविंदाय गोपालाय नमः ॥

Transliteration:
Om Shreem Shreem Krishnaaya Govindaya Gopaalaya Namah

Meaning:
"O Krishna, the embodiment of joy, O Govinda, the sustainer of the world, O Gopala, the protector of all beings, I bow to You with devotion!"

Chapter 9 – Shattila Ekadashi: The Sesame of Purity 🌿

🌷 The Day of Sacred Seeds — Shattila Ekadashi

- **English Name:** Shattila Ekadashi
- **Hindi Name:** षट्तिला एकादशी
- **Pronunciation:** Shaṭṭilā Ekādaśī

📅 Tithi and Timing

• **Hindu Calendar Tithi:** Māgha Krishna Paksha Ekadashi (माघ कृष्ण पक्ष एकादशी)

• **Approximate Gregorian Calendar Timing:** January–February

🌙 Astronomical Note:

During the dark half of the moon (Krishna Paksha), the body naturally eliminates toxins. Fasting on Shattila Ekadashi strengthens this purification process, aligning inner and outer cleansings.

✿ Significance of Shattila Ekadashi

The word "Shattila" means "Six Uses of Sesame" (Shaṭ = six, Tilā = sesame).
This Ekadashi emphasizes purifying the body, mind, and karma by using sesame seeds (Til) in six sacred ways:

- Bathing with sesame-infused water,
- Rubbing the body with sesame paste,
- Offering sesame into the fire (havan),
- Donating sesame,
- Eating sesame preparations,
- Performing water oblations with sesame.

Sesame is no ordinary seed — it is considered sacred, linked with Saturn (Shani) and divine energy, known to absorb negativity and bestow long life.
Thus, observing Shattila Ekadashi is seen as a way to dissolve hidden karmic debts and cultivate purity.

The Story of Shattila Ekadashi

Yudhishthira asked Lord Krishna:
"O Lord! What is the name of the *Ekadashi* that falls in the *Krishna Paksha* (the waning phase of the moon) of the month of *Magha* (January–February)? What are its procedures and benefits? Kindly explain everything to me in detail."

Lord Krishna replied:
"O King! The *Ekadashi* of *Krishna Paksha* in the month of *Magha* is known as *Shattila Ekadashi* (literally 'Six-Sesame Ekadashi'). It is renowned for destroying all sins. Now, listen to the sin-destroying story that the sage *Pulastya* (a revered ancient sage or *rishi*) told to *Dalbhya* (another sage)."

Dalbhya asked Pulastya:
"O great sage! In the world of mortals, people often commit sinful actions. Please tell me a way by which they can avoid going to *Naraka* (hell or lower worlds in Hindu cosmology)."

Pulastya replied:
"O noble one! When the month of *Magha* arrives, a person should bathe and purify themselves, practice *indriya-samyam* (self-restraint of the senses), and give up vices such as *kama* (lust), *krodha* (anger), *ahankara* (ego), *lobha* (greed), and *ninda* (gossip or slander). While remembering *Devadideva* (the Lord of Lords, a name for Lord Vishnu), they should wash their feet and gather cow dung from the ground (used in traditional rituals for its symbolic purity).

Then, mix *til* (sesame seeds) and cotton into the dung and make 108 balls from it (108 being a sacred number in Hinduism). When the

Ashlesha or *Moola Nakshatra* (specific lunar constellations in Hindu astrology) appears in *Magha*, one should take a vow (*niyama*) to observe the *Ekadashi* fast.

After thoroughly bathing and purifying oneself, worship *Devadideva Sri Vishnu* (Lord Vishnu, the preserver god in the Hindu trinity) with a pure heart. If any mistake occurs, chant the name of Lord Krishna. Stay awake all night (*jagaran*) and perform sacred fire rituals (*homa*). Worship Lord *Hari* (another name for Vishnu), who holds a *shankha* (conch), *chakra* (discus), and *gada* (mace), using sandalwood paste, *arghya* (ritual offering), camphor, and food offerings (*naivedya*).

Then, while remembering the Lord and chanting His name, offer fruits like pumpkin, coconut, or *bijora* (a citrus fruit) as a ritual gift (*arghya*). If these items are unavailable, one can also use 100 betel nuts for worship and offering. The *arghya mantra* (prayer said during offering) is as follows:

Arghya Mantra:

Kṛṣṇa Kṛṣṇa Kṛpālu tvaṁ agatīnām gatirbhava |
Saṁsārārṇava magnānāṁ prasīda puruṣottama ||
Namaḥ te puṇḍarīkākṣa namaḥ te viśvabhāvana

|
Suhṛdāṁ namaste'stu mahāpuruṣa pūrvaja ||
Gṛhāṇārghyaṁ mayā dattaṁ Lakṣmyā saha jagatpate ||

[Translation of the Mantra]:
"O Krishna, embodiment of compassion, you are the savior of the helpless. We are drowning in the ocean of worldly existence—please show us mercy, O Supreme Person. Salutations to you, O lotus-eyed one (*Pundarīkākṣa*), Creator of the Universe (*Viśvabhāvana*), Friend of all (*Suhṛt*), Great and Primordial Being (*Mahāpuruṣa Pūrva-ja*)! O Lord of the Universe (*Jagatpati*), kindly accept this offering (*arghya*) made by me along with Goddess Lakshmi (your divine consort)."

After that, worship a *Brahmin* (a member of the priestly class in Hindu society) and offer him a pot of water, an umbrella, shoes, and clothes (*vastra*). While making the offering, say:
"May Lord Krishna be pleased with me through this donation."

According to one's ability, donate a black cow (*krishna-gau*) to a worthy Brahmin. O noble one, a learned person should also donate a pot full of sesame seeds. The number of branches that grow from these seeds represents the number of thousands of years the donor will reside in *Svargaloka* (heavenly realm in Hindu cosmology).

One should also bathe using sesame seeds, use sesame in fire offerings (*homa*), apply sesame paste to the body, drink water mixed with sesame, donate sesame, and cook food with sesame.

Thus, O King, because sesame (*til*) is used in six different ways in this observance, this *Ekadashi* is called Shat-Tila Ekadashi (*'shat' meaning six, and 'tila' meaning sesame*), and it is known to destroy all sins.

ॐ Meditation

At sunrise, sit calmly with your gaze softly focused ahead.
Begin to listen — not to any sound, but to the space between sounds.
Let your awareness rest in this gap, this silence, as if it were a presence.
Silently affirm:
"*In stillness between sounds, I hear the voice of the infinite.*"
This meditation, called Shabdantar Dhyana (Meditation on the Gap Between Sounds),

awakens awareness of the subtle dimension of existence.

Mantra

Sanskrit:
शांताकारं भुजगशयनं पद्मनाभं सुरेशं ।
विश्वाधारं गगनसदृशं मेघवर्णं शुभाङ्गम् ॥

Transliteration:
Śāntākāraṃ Bhujagaśayanaṃ Padmanābhaṃ Sureśam,
Viśvādhāraṃ Gaganasadṛśaṃ Meghavarṇaṃ Śubhāṅgam.

Meaning:
"I bow to Vishnu, the peaceful One, who rests upon the serpent, the lotus-naveled Lord of all gods, the support of the universe, boundless as the sky, cloud-hued and beautiful".

Chapter 10 — Jaya Ekadashi: Victory of the Spirit 🌿

🏵️ The Day of Inner Triumph — Jaya Ekadashi

- **English Name**: Jaya Ekadashi
- **Hindi Name**: जया एकादशी
- **Pronunciation**: Jayā Ekādaśī

📅 Tithi and Timing

• **Hindu Calendar Tithi:** Māgha Shukla Paksha Ekadashi (माघ शुक्ल पक्ष एकादशी)

• **Approximate Gregorian Calendar Timing:** February–March

🌙 Astronomical Note:

During the waxing moon (Shukla Paksha), the body's vital energies (*ojas*, or subtle essence of life) are believed to strengthen naturally in Hindu and yogic tradition. Fasting at this phase is said to enhance mental clarity and spiritual receptivity.

The Story of Jaya Ekadashi: A Tale from Indra's Court

Yudhishthira asked Lord Shri Krishna:
"O Lord! Please kindly tell me—what is the name of the Ekadashi (11th lunar day, considered highly sacred in Hinduism) that falls in the Shukla Paksha (bright fortnight, i.e., waxing phase of the moon) of the month of Magha (January–February in the Hindu calendar)? What is the method of its observance, and which deity is worshipped on that day?"

Lord Shri Krishna said:
"O King! The Ekadashi that falls in the bright half of the month of Magha is called 'Jaya'. It is a supreme tithi (sacred lunar day) that removes all sins. Being pure in itself, it destroys sins and grants both fortune (material and spiritual prosperity) and liberation (moksha, i.e., freedom from the cycle of rebirth) to human beings. Not only that—it also destroys great sins like Brahma-hatya (killing a Brahmin, considered one of the most heinous sins) and relieves one from the curse of becoming a ghost (pishacha, a restless and tormented spirit). By observing its vrat (religious fast and vow), people never fall into hellish births. Therefore, O King! One

should diligently observe the vow of this Ekadashi named 'Jaya'.

Once, in Svargaloka (heaven, the celestial realm of the gods), King Indra (king of the devas or gods) was ruling. The gods were enjoying in Nandana forest (divine pleasure garden of heaven) among Parijat trees (heavenly flowering trees) with celestial maidens (apsaras, divine dancers). Indra, lord of fifty crore Gandharvas (celestial musicians), organized a grand dance performance for pleasure while freely enjoying the forest. Gandharvas were singing—among them, Pushpadanta, Chitrasena, and his son were the main ones. Chitrasena's wife was named Malini, and from her a daughter was born, known as Pushpavanti. Pushpadanta had a son named Malyavan, who was deeply attracted to Pushpavanti's beauty. Both of them came to perform the dance for Indra's satisfaction.

As the singing began, they were accompanied by apsaras. Due to mutual affection, both Malyavan and Pushpavanti became overcome by infatuation. Disruption occurred in the performance; their singing became disorganized. Sometimes the rhythm was broken; sometimes the song halted altogether.

Indra took notice of this distraction, felt insulted, and became angry.

Hence, cursing them both, he said:
"O fools! Shame upon you! You have fallen and disobeyed my command. Therefore, becoming husband and wife, you shall be born as pishachas (ghosts, disembodied spirits who suffer due to past misdeeds)!"

After receiving this dreadful curse, the two were overwhelmed with sorrow. They went to the Himalayas and, having taken birth as pishachas, began to suffer terrible misery. Tormented by the pain arising from their ghostly bodies, they wandered among the caves of the mountains.

One day, the male ghost said to his ghost-wife: "What sin have we committed that we have attained this pishacha birth? Hell is extremely terrible, and this ghostly existence is also full of suffering. Hence, we must make full effort to rid ourselves of sin."

Thus, absorbed in such thoughts and overwhelmed by suffering, they became emaciated. By divine arrangement, they came upon the Ekadashi of the Shukla Paksha in Magha month. Known by the name 'Jaya', that tithi is supreme among all tithis (sacred lunar days). On that day, they gave up all kinds of food, not even drinking water. They committed no violence towards any living being—not even plucking fruits to eat. Continually tormented by sorrow, they sat near a Peepal tree (sacred fig tree, considered especially holy in Hinduism).

The sun set, and the terrifying night, which takes away life, approached. They did not sleep, nor did they experience any comfort or joy.

As the sun rose and it became Dwadashi (the 12th lunar day, the day after Ekadashi), their observance of 'Jaya' Ekadashi was complete. They had even remained awake through the night (a key part of the observance, known as jagaran). Due to the effect of this vrat and the power of Lord Vishnu (the preserver deity of the Hindu trinity), their ghostly forms were destroyed. Pushpavanti and Malyavan regained their original forms. The same affection as before filled their hearts. Their bodies once again became adorned with beautiful ornaments.

Taking on charming forms, they boarded a celestial airplane (vimana) and ascended to Svargaloka (heaven). There, they approached

Indra and offered him respectful obeisance with great joy.

Seeing them in such a form, Indra was greatly astonished! He asked:
"Tell me, by what meritorious act were you freed from your ghostly existence? You had surely been cursed by me—then which deity has liberated you?"

Malyavan replied:
"O Lord! By the grace of Lord Vasudeva (another name of Lord Krishna or Vishnu) and the observance of the Ekadashi named 'Jaya', our pishacha condition has been removed."

Then Indra said:
"...Now, by my order, both of you may drink sudha (nectar of the gods, also called amrita, which grants immortality). Those who are devoted to the observance of Ekadashi and who surrender to Lord Shri Krishna are worthy of our worship."

Lord Shri Krishna concluded:
"O King! For this reason, one must observe Ekadashi. O ruler of men! The 'Jaya' Ekadashi even removes the sin of Brahma-hatya (killing of a Brahmin). Whoever observes the vow of 'Jaya' has given all kinds of charity and has performed all the yajnas (Vedic sacrificial

rituals). Reading or hearing this glory gives the merit equal to that of performing an Agnistoma Yajna (a major Vedic fire sacrifice, considered one of the most meritorious rituals)."

ॐ Meditation

Sit in stillness.
Instead of reciting a mantra aloud, listen silently within yourself – feel the sound arising and dissolving like a soft ocean wave.
Observe the space between breaths, between heartbeats.
Dissolve into that infinite space.
"In the gap between two sounds, realization blossoms".

Mantra

Sanskrit:

जयन्ती मङ्गला काली भद्रकाली कपालिनी ।
दुर्गा क्षमा शिवा धात्री स्वाहा स्वधा नमोऽस्तु ते ॥

Transliteration:

Jayantī Maṅgalā Kālī Bhadrakālī Kapālinī,
Durgā Kṣamā Śivā Dhātrī Svāhā Svadha
Namo'stu Te.

Meaning:

"Salutations to You, O Victory-bestowing Divine Mother, who is auspicious, fierce, and compassionate!"

Chapter 11 — Vijaya Ekadashi: Triumph Over Adversities 🌿

🏵 The Day of Divine Victory — Vijaya Ekadashi

- **English Name**: Vijaya Ekadashi
- **Hindi Name**: विजया एकादशी
- **Pronunciation**: Vih-juh-yah Eh-kah-duh-shee

📅 Tithi and Timing 🌷

• **Hindu Calendar Tithi**: Phalguna Krishna Paksha Ekadashi (फाल्गुन कृष्ण पक्ष एकादशी)

• **Approximate Gregorian Calendar Timing**: February–March

🌙 Astronomical Note:

During the Krishna Paksha (waning phase of the moon), the body's energies naturally turn inward. Observing a fast during this time supports deep detoxification and emotional purification.

The Story of Vijaya Ekadashi

Yudhishthir asked: "O Vasudev! In the Krishna Paksha (the dark fortnight, or the second half of the lunar month) of Phalgun (according to Gujarat Maharat, this corresponds to Magh), which Ekadashi occurs, and what is the procedure for observing it? Please kindly explain."

Lord Krishna replied: "Yudhishthir! Once, Naradji (a celestial sage in Hinduism) asked Lord Brahma (the creator god in Hinduism) about the merits of the Vijay Ekadashi (the 'Victory' Ekadashi observed in the Krishna Paksha of Phalgun), and Lord Brahma narrated the story and procedure of this Ekadashi to him. Listen carefully:

Lord Brahma said: "Narad! This Ekadashi is very ancient, auspicious, and destroys sins. It bestows victory to kings, and there is no doubt about it. In the Treta Yuga (the second age in the Hindu cycle of four Yugas), when Lord Ramchandra (an incarnation of the god Vishnu, known for his victory over the demon king Ravana) reached the shores of the ocean to attack Lanka (the island kingdom of the demon king Ravana), he found no way to cross it. He asked Lord Laxman (his devoted brother), 'O Lakshman! By which method can this ocean be crossed? It is extremely deep and filled with dangerous creatures. I do not see any way to cross it easily.'

Lakshman replied: 'O Lord! You are the original divine being and the eternal person, Purushottam (the supreme person, a title used for Lord Ram in Hinduism). What is hidden from you? Half a yojana (a traditional Hindu unit of measurement, roughly 8 miles) from here, on the Kumari Island, lives the ancient sage Bakdalbhya. You should go to him and ask for a solution.'

Lord Ramchandra went to the great sage Bakdalbhya and bowed to him. The sage, after greeting Lord Ramchandra, asked the reason for his visit.

Lord Ramchandra said: 'O Sage! I have come with my army to attack Lanka. Please tell me the way to cross this ocean.'

The sage Bakdalbhya replied: 'O Ramchandra! In the Krishna Paksha of Phalgun, there is an Ekadashi called 'Vijaya' ('Victory'). By observing the fast on this Ekadashi, you will achieve victory. Certainly, you will be able to cross the ocean with your vanara (monkey) army. Now listen to the beneficial procedure for observing this fast:

On the day of Dashami (the tenth day of the lunar calendar), establish a kalash (a sacred vessel, often filled with water or offerings) made of gold, silver, copper, or clay, fill it with water, and place leaves in it. On top of it, establish the idol of Lord Narayan (a name for Lord Vishnu, the preserver of the universe) in a golden form. On the Ekadashi day, after taking a ritual bath at dawn, re-establish the kalash. Worship it specially with a garland, sandalwood, betel nuts, and coconut. Place barley and grains on the kalash, and offer incense, a lamp, and various food offerings. Spend the day in the service of the kalash, listening to stories and singing praises. At night, keep vigil (Jagran, a ritual of staying awake and singing or chanting in devotion) in front of the kalash, lighting a ghee (clarified butter) lamp for an unbroken fast. The next morning, at sunrise, place the kalash near a water source (river, lake, or pond), perform its ritualistic worship, and donate it with devotion to a learned Brahmin (a priest or scholar, highly respected in Hindu society). Along with the kalash, donate other significant items. O Ram! You should observe this 'Vijaya Ekadashi' fast with your army. By doing so, you will be victorious.'

Lord Brahma says: Narad! Upon hearing this, Lord Ramchandra followed the sage's instructions and observed the 'Vijaya Ekadashi' fast. As a result, he became victorious. He killed Ravana (the demon king of Lanka), conquered Lanka, and rescued Sita (his wife, kidnapped by Ravana). O son! Those who observe this fast in this manner attain victory in this world, and their afterlife remains eternal.

Lord Krishna says: Yudhishthir! Therefore, the 'Vijaya' fast should be observed. By reading or listening to this story, one receives the benefits of performing a Rajasuya Yajna (a great Vedic sacrifice, usually performed by kings to establish their authority and righteousness).
Thus, Vijaya Ekadashi carries the power to grant success in even the most impossible endeavors".

✿ Meditation

Close your eyes and visualize Lord Vishnu standing gloriously in the cosmic ocean, radiating infinite light and compassion.
Focus gently on the heart center and mentally chant:
"Om Vijayaaya Namah" — "Salutations to the

One Who Grants Victory."
"Imagine yourself riding a golden chariot across the inner sky of your mind, driven by the will of the Divine. As you dissolve into the vastness, feel all obstacles melting into the ocean of pure consciousness".

ॐ Mantra

Sanskrit:
ॐ नमो भगवते रामचन्द्राय नमः

Transliteration:

"Om Namo Bhagavate Ramachandraya Namah"
Meaning:

"Salutations to Lord Rama, the embodiment of divine victory and righteousness."

Chapter 12 — Amalaki Ekadashi: The Grace of the Divine Fruit 🌿

🏵 The Day of Sacred Blessings — Amalaki Ekadashi

- **English Name**: Amalaki Ekadashi
- **Hindi Name**: आमलकी एकादशी
- **Pronunciation**: Aa-ma-la-kee Eh-kah-da-shee

📅 Tithi and Timing

- **Hindu Calendar Tithi**: Phalguna Shukla Paksha Ekadashi (फाल्गुन शुक्ल पक्ष एकादशी)
- **Gregorian Calendar Timing**: Falls in February–March

🏵 Significance of Amalaki Ekadashi

Amalaki (Amla or Indian gooseberry) is celebrated for its spiritual and medicinal significance. In Hindu tradition, the day is observed with worship of both the **Amalaki tree** and **Lord Vishnu**, believed to dwell within the tree during this Ekadashi.

✿ Story of Amalaki Ekadashi

Yudhishthira (eldest of the Pandava brothers in the Mahabharata, known for his righteousness) said to Lord Shri Krishna (a major deity in Hinduism, considered the Supreme Being by Vaishnavas):
"Shri Krishna! Please be kind enough to tell me the name and significance of the *Ekadashi* (the 11th lunar day in the Hindu calendar, observed as a day of fasting and devotion) that falls in the *Shukla Paksha* (the waxing phase of the moon) of the month of *Phalguna* (February-March in the Gregorian calendar)."

Lord Shri Krishna said:
"O highly fortunate one, delight of *Dharma* (righteousness or moral duty)! The name of the *Ekadashi* in the *Shukla Paksha* of *Phalguna* is *Amalaki* (also called Amla or Indian Gooseberry, a sacred tree in Hinduism). Observing this vow leads one to *Vishnuloka* (the divine abode of Lord Vishnu, a heavenly realm). King *Mandhata* (a legendary righteous king from Hindu mythology) once asked the sage *Vasishtha* (one of the seven great sages,

or *Saptarishi*) the same question. *Vasishtha* replied:

"O highly fortunate one! When *Lord Vishnu* (the Preserver in the Hindu Trinity—*Trimurti*) once spat, a radiant drop, shining like the moon, emerged from His mouth and fell upon the Earth. From that spot grew the great *Amalaka* tree (*Phyllanthus emblica*, revered in Hindu tradition), which is considered the original among all trees. At that time, to establish ritual worship, the Lord created *Brahmaji* (the creator god in Hinduism), who then gave birth to various beings: gods (*Devas*), demons (*Danavas*), celestial musicians (*Gandharvas*), nature spirits (*Yakshas*), demons (*Rakshasas*), serpent beings (*Nagas*), and wise sages (*Mahishis*) with pure hearts. Among them, the gods and sages came to the place where the sacred *Amalaka* tree stood. O fortunate one! Seeing it, they were filled with wonder, for they had never seen such a tree before.

As they stood in amazement, a divine voice (*Akashvani* – a celestial oraclesque voice from the sky) said:
'O sages! This is the supreme *Amalaka* tree, which is very dear to *Vishnu*. Merely remembering it grants the merit (*Punya*) equal

to donating a cow (*Godana*), worshipping it yields double that merit, and eating its fruit grants triple merit. This is a sacred *Vaishnava* (relating to *Vishnu*) tree that destroys all sins. At its root resides *Vishnu*, above Him *Brahma*, in the trunk *Rudra* (another name for *Shiva*, the Destroyer in the Hindu Trinity), in the branches the sages (*Munis*), in the twigs the gods (*Devas*), in the leaves the elemental deities (*Vasus*), in the flowers the storm gods (*Maruts*), and in the fruits reside all the respected deities (*Pujyapitas*). The *Amalaka* tree embodies all the gods. Therefore, it is supremely holy for *Vishnu*-devotees and should always be consumed with reverence.'

The sages asked: "Who are you? A god or someone else? Please tell us clearly."

Then the divine voice replied:
"I am the eternal *Vishnu*, the controller of all beings (*Bhutas*) and the ruler of all worlds (*Bhavanas*), whom even the wisest (*Vijnana Purushas*) struggle to perceive."

Upon hearing this, the sages began praising *Lord Vishnu*. Pleased, *Shri Hari* (another name for *Vishnu*, meaning "Remover of sins") said: "O sages! What boon (*Var*) shall I grant you?"

The sages replied:
"Lord! If you are pleased, please tell us of a *Vrata* (a sacred religious observance or vow) that grants both *Svarga* (heaven) and *Moksha* (liberation from the cycle of rebirth)."

Shri Vishnu said:
"O sages! If the *Ekadashi* in the Shukla Paksha of *Phalguna* coincides with a *Punya Nakshatra* (an auspicious lunar constellation), then it becomes a powerful destroyer of sins and bestower of great merit. On that day, one should keep vigil (*Jagaran*) at night near the *Amalaka* tree. This frees one from all sins and brings the merit equal to donating a thousand cows. O sages! Among all vows, this one is the highest, which I have now shared with you."

The sages asked:
"Lord! Please describe the procedure of this *Vrata*. Who is its presiding deity? What are the *Mantras* (sacred chants)? How should the worship (*Puja*) be performed? What is the method for bathing and charity?"

Shri Vishnu said:
"O sages! On this *Ekadashi*, one should rise early in the morning, brush the teeth, and take a vow (*Sankalpa*) saying:
'O *Pundarikaksha* (lotus-eyed one)! O *Achyuta* (the infallible)! I shall fast on this *Ekadashi* and

eat the next day. Please protect me.'
After this, avoid contact with fallen people, thieves, heretics, immoral persons, those who insult gurus (*Gurudrohis*), and those who break moral boundaries. Bathe in a river, pond, well, or at home with discipline. Before bathing, apply sacred mud (*Mridika*).

Mantra for applying mud:
"*Arbante rathabante Vishnubante Vasundhare, Mridike har me paapam janmakotiyam samarchitam.*"
(O Earth, who bears chariots and warriors, who was measured by *Vishnu* during His *Vamana* incarnation — O sacred mud! Please destroy my sins accumulated over millions of births.)

Mantra for bathing:
"*Tvam matah sarvabhutanam jivanam tvam rakshakam...*
Snato'ham sarvatirtheshu..."
(O Goddess of water! You are the life and protector of all beings. You are the mistress of all tastes. I have bathed in all sacred rivers, lakes, and divine ponds. May this bath be the fruit of all holy baths.)

A learned person should create a golden idol of *Parashurama* (the warrior-sage and sixth incarnation of *Vishnu*) according to his capacity (either full or half a *masha* — a traditional measure of gold). After the bath, return home and perform rituals like *Puja* and *Havan* (fire offering). Then, gather offerings and proceed to the *Amalaka* tree. Clean the area and sanctify it.

Place a new water pot (*Kalasha*) filled with water, *Panchamrita* (a mixture of milk, curd, ghee, honey, and sugar), and fragrances. Apply white sandalwood paste, adorn it with a flower garland, and light lamps and incense. Decorate the place with beauty and reverence. Bring a new umbrella, footwear, and garments.

Place *Akshata* (uncooked rice) on a plate on top of the *Kalasha*, and install the idol of *Parashurama*.

Mantras for worship (each mantra corresponds to a body part):

- "Vishokaya Namah" - feet
- "Vishnuroopine Namah" - knees
- "Umaya Namah" - thighs
- "Damodaraya Namah" - waist
- "Padmanabhaya Namah" - abdomen
- "Shrivatsadharine Namah" - chest
- "Chibane Namah" - left arm

- "Gadine Namah" – right arm
- "Vaikunthaya Namah" – neck
- "Yajnamukhaya Namah" – face
- "Vishokinadhaye Namah" – nose
- "Vasudevaya Namah" – eyes
- "Vamanaya Namah" – forehead
- "Sarvatmane Namah" – entire body and head

After that, offer *Arghya* (ritual offering with water and fruits) to Lord *Parashurama* with this mantra:
"*Namaste Devadevesha Jamadagnya Namo'stu Te,*
Grihanarghyamimam Drishtam Amalakya Yutam Hare."
(O Lord of gods, son of *Jamadagni*, form of *Vishnu*, *Parashurama*! Please accept this *Arghya* offered along with *Amalaka* fruit.)

Then, stay awake (*Jagaran*) the whole night, engaging in devotional singing (*Kirtan*), dancing, storytelling (*Katha*), and discussions about *Vishnu*. Circumambulate (*Parikrama*) the *Amalaka* tree 108 or 28 times while chanting *Vishnu*'s names.

At dawn, perform *Aarti* (ritual waving of light), worship a *Brahmin* (priest or spiritual teacher), and donate all items used in worship.

Donate the *Kalasha*, garments, shoes, and other offerings, praying:
"May *Vishnu*, in the form of *Parashurama*, be pleased with me."

Touch the *Amalaka* tree, perform circumambulation, bathe again, and respectfully feed *Brahmins*. After that, eat with family.

The merit earned from visiting all holy sites (*Tirthas*) and giving all forms of charity (*Dana*) is attained by observing this *Vrata*. It even surpasses the fruits of all sacrifices (*Yajnas*). There is no doubt that this is the supreme vow among all.

Vasishtha concluded:
"O King! After narrating this, *Lord Vishnu* disappeared. Then all the sages followed this *Vrata* strictly. O best of kings! You too must observe this vow in the same way."

Lord Shri Krishna said:
"Yudhishthira! This sacred vow (*Vrata*) liberates humans from all sins."

Ritual Observances

Devotees wake early, bathe, and offer fruits, flowers, turmeric, and incense to the Amalaki tree. The main mantra chanted on this day is:

"Om Namo Bhagavate Vasudevaya" (ॐ नमो भगवते वासुदेवाय)

Meaning: "I bow to Vasudeva, the all-pervading Divinity."

They also perform pradakshina (circumambulation) of the tree while reciting Vishnu's names and meditating on divine light and healing.

Meditation

A visual meditation involves imagining a radiant golden Amalaki tree rooted at the heart center. Its light expands outward, filling the mind and body with healing energy. Chant:

"Om Amrtaaya Namah" – "Salutations to the Lord of Divine Nectar."

Chapter 13 — Pāpamocanī Ekādaśī: The Day of Removing the Sins 🌿

🏵 The Remover of Sins — Pāpamocanī Ekādaśī

- **English Name**: Papmochani Ekadashi
- **Hindi Name**: पापमोचनी एकादशी
- **Pronunciation**: Paap-mo-cha-nee Eh-kaa-da-shee

📅 Tithi and Timing

• **Hindu Calendar Tithi**: Chaitra Krishna Paksha Ekadashi (चैत्र कृष्ण पक्ष एकादशी)

• **Approximate Gregorian Calendar Timing**: March–April

🌙 Astronomical Note:

This Ekadashi occurs during the waning moon phase, traditionally associated with purification, introspection, and karmic resolution.

✿ The Sacred Tale of Pāpamocanī Ekādaśī

King Yudhishthira once asked Lord Shri Krishna about the Ekadashi that falls in the dark fortnight (Krishna Paksha – the waning phase of the moon) of the month of Chaitra (March–April in the Hindu calendar; in the Gujarat tradition, it corresponds to the month of Phalguna or February–March). He said:

"O Lord! I wish to know about the Ekadashi of this fortnight—its name, procedure, and the merit one attains from observing it. Kindly explain all these details to me."

Lord Krishna replied:

"O King! I shall narrate to you a sin-destroying legend which was once told by the great sage Lomasha to the noble king Mandhata when he inquired about the same."

King Mandhata had asked:

"O Bhagavan (a respectful title for God or a divine sage)! I desire to hear this for the welfare of the people. What is the name of the Ekadashi that falls in the dark half of the month of Chaitra? What is its procedure, and what fruits (spiritual benefits) does it bestow?"

Sage Lomasha said:

"O King! In ancient times, in a forest named Chaitraratha—served by celestial nymphs (Apsaras, divine female beings known for their beauty and dancing), and where the daughters of the Gandharvas (celestial musicians) played instruments and sang songs—there lived a beautiful apsara named Manjughosha. She once attempted to seduce the sage Medhavi, who was residing there and engaged in strict tapasya (austerity, penance for spiritual growth).

Out of fear of the sage, Manjughosha stayed a kosha (an ancient Indian unit of distance, roughly 2 miles or 3.2 kilometers) away from his hermitage and began to sing melodiously while playing the veena (a traditional Indian string instrument). The sage, while wandering, came across her and was overwhelmed by kama (desire/lust) upon seeing her beauty and hearing her music. Manjughosha then approached him and embraced him, and the sage succumbed to her charms.

They lived together in indulgence, completely unaware of day and night. Time passed, and many days went by in this manner. When Manjughosha eventually wished to return to the Devaloka (the heavenly realm of the gods), she said:

'O Sage! Please permit me to go back to my abode.'

The sage replied:

'Dear one, stay with me until the Brahma Muhurta (the pre-dawn period considered spiritually significant).'

To this, Manjughosha responded:

'O wise one! Countless twilights have already passed! Kindly reflect on how much time has gone by.'

Hearing this, Sage Medhavi was startled and began calculating the time that had passed. He realized that he had wasted 57 years with her, thus ruining his penance. Enraged, he cursed her:

'You sinful woman! Become a pishachi (a type of female demon or ghost in Hindu mythology).'

Afflicted by the curse, Manjughosha bowed humbly and said:

'O Sage! Please free me from this curse. It is said that even walking seven steps with a noble person forms a sacred bond. I have spent many years with you. O Lord! Have mercy on me.'

The sage said:

'What can I do now? You have caused the ruin of my great tapasya (penance). Yet, listen. The Ekadashi that falls in the dark half of the month of Chaitra is known as Papamochani Ekadashi (*Papa* means "sin", and *Mochani* means "that which frees or removes"). Observing the vrata (religious fast or vow) of this Ekadashi destroys all sins and will free you from the curse of becoming a pishachi.'

Having said this, the sage returned to the hermitage of his father, the great sage Chyavana. Upon seeing his son, Chyavana asked:

'My son, what have you done? You have destroyed your accumulated punya (spiritual merit)!'

Sage Medhavi replied:

'Father! I have committed a great sin by engaging with an apsara. Kindly tell me a way to atone for this.'

Chyavana said:

'My son! By observing the Papamochani Ekadashi, which falls in the dark fortnight of Chaitra, all accumulated sins are destroyed.'

Hearing this, Medhavi observed the fast with full devotion. As a result, all his sins were destroyed, and he once again became full of spiritual power. Manjughosha too performed the Papamochani Ekadashi vrata and was freed from her demonic form. She regained her divine beauty and returned to the celestial realms.

Lord Shri Krishna concluded:

"O King! Anyone who observes the Papamochani Ekadashi is freed from all sins. Simply reading or listening to the glory of this Ekadashi grants the merit of donating a thousand cows (considered one of the highest acts of charity in Hinduism).

✿ Meditation

Visualize a gentle golden light descending from above, washing away guilt and sorrow. In your heart's eye, see Lord Vishnu smiling compassionately, inviting you into peace and purity.

ॐ Mantra

Sanskrit:

अपि चेत्सुदुराचारो भजते मामनन्यभाक्।
साधुरेव स मन्तव्यः सम्यग्व्यवसितो हि सः॥

Transliteration:

api cet su-durācāro bhajate mām ananya-bhāk
sādhur eva sa mantavyaḥ samyag vyavasito hi saḥ

Meaning:

"Even if one commits the most grievous acts, if they worship Me with exclusive devotion, they must be regarded as righteous."

Chapter 14 — Kamada Ekādaśī: The Fulfillment of Every Wish

The Day of Wish-Fulfillment — Kamada Ekādaśī

- **English Name:** Kamada Ekadashi
- **Hindi Name:** कामदा एकादशी
- **Pronunciation:** *Kaa-ma-da Eh-kaa-da-shee*

Tithi and Timing

- **Hindu Calendar Tithi:** Chaitra Shukla Paksha Ekadashi (चैत्र शुक्ल पक्ष एकादशी)
- **Approximate Gregorian Calendar Timing:** March–April

Astronomical Note:

This Ekadashi occurs during the waxing moon phase, where energy is expansive and nurturing. It aligns with the body's biological renewal cycle, assisting physical rejuvenation and emotional upliftment.

✿ The Divine Story of Kamada Ekādaśī

Yudhishthira asked: Vasudev! I bow to you! Please, tell me, which Ekadashi occurs in the Chaitra Shukla Paksha?

Lord Krishna replied: O King! Listen closely to this ancient and captivating story, one that Vashishtha (a revered sage and one of the seven great rishis in Hindu tradition) once shared when King Dilip (an ancient Indian king, known for his wisdom and courage) asked him a similar question.

Vashishtha said: O King! In the Chaitra Shukla Paksha (the waxing phase of the moon during the month of Chaitra, which typically falls around March-April), a powerful and mysterious Ekadashi appears, known as *Kamada*. It is not just an auspicious day, but a day that holds the power to vanquish sins and grant divine grace. For those caught in the web of life's deepest wrongs, it is like a blazing fire that consumes the forest of their misdeeds.

The ancient tale unfolds: In a distant land, hidden in a forgotten corner of the world, lay a stunning city called Nagpur (city of serpents). It was a city of unimaginable wealth. In this magnificent city, the mighty serpent *Pundarik* (a powerful, divine serpent) ruled. His presence was so imposing that even the bravest beings dared not cross his path. Along with him lived creatures of the highest realms—Gandharvas (celestial musicians whose songs could stir the heavens), kinnars (mythical beings with both human and divine traits), and apsaras (celestial nymphs, known for their beauty and charm).

Among them, there was one apsara named *Lalita*, known for her grace and allure. She was accompanied by the Gandharva *Lalit*, her husband. They were trapped in a strange, forbidden bond. Lalita's heart constantly pulsed with thoughts of her husband, while Lalit's thoughts were consumed by the enchanting beauty of Lalita. A deep, mysterious longing, full of love, echoed in their souls.

One fateful day, as King Pundarik sat in his royal court, a sudden disturbance struck. Lalit, the Gandharva, was singing his song in the court, but something was wrong—his beloved Lalita was not by his side. As the melody rose and fell, something stirred in Lalit's heart. He suddenly felt the absence of Lalita, and in an instant, his body froze. His tongue, once fluid with music, stumbled into silence.

Another serpent *Karkotak* sensed the change in Lalit and rushed to inform King Pundarik. As soon as the serpent king heard of this sorrowful shift, his eyes blazed with fiery anger. His voice, like thunder, boomed across the court: "You, foolish one! How dare you fall victim to the charms of your wife while in my presence? I curse you! Become a demon and suffer the consequences of your desires!"

In the blink of an eye, Lalit was transformed. His divine form twisted into something terrifying. His face contorted into a monster's, his eyes burning with fury, and his entire being radiated dread. No longer a Gandharva, he had become a demon.

Lalita, watching her husband's transformation, felt her world crumble. Her heart was torn with grief and confusion. What could she do? How could she save her husband from this curse?

Desperate for answers, Lalita fled into the deep, dark forests, trailing behind her husband. The dense trees whispered secrets of the ancient world as she journeyed deeper into the wilderness. There, in a hidden clearing, she stumbled upon an ashram (a secluded spiritual retreat, often associated with sages and divine wisdom), bathed in an ethereal glow. In the heart of the ashram, a sage sat in deep meditation. He seemed untouched by the chaos of the world, his mind at peace with the universe.

Lalita, with reverence and awe, approached the sage. She bowed low before him and stood, waiting. The sage, sensing the weight of her sorrow, opened his eyes, which gleamed with ancient knowledge. His voice was like a gentle breeze: "O blessed one! Who are you, and why have you come to me in such distress? Tell me your story."

Lalita, desperate for guidance, explained: "Great sage, I am the daughter of *Viradhanva* (a Gandharva of renown). My name is Lalita. My husband has been cursed and transformed into a demon due to his own sins. I cannot bear to see him suffer in this form. O sage, tell me what I must do! What penance (a spiritual practice to atone for sins) must I perform to redeem him? Show me the way."

The sage, his voice filled with compassion and wisdom, spoke with the calmness of a thousand lifetimes: "O sorrowful one, do not despair. The day of *Kamada Ekadashi* has arrived in this Chaitra month, during the Shukla Paksha. This Ekadashi is known to destroy the gravest of sins and is a powerful remedy for all misdeeds. If you observe this Ekadashi with full devotion and offer the merits of your fast to your husband, his curse will be lifted, and he will be freed from his demonic state."

Vashishtha says: Upon hearing these words, Lalita's heart filled with hope. She vowed to fast on the sacred Ekadashi, determined to save her husband from the grip of his curse. On the day of the Ekadashi, she stood before Lord Vasudev (a name for Lord Krishna, the supreme god in Hinduism), praying with all her heart. She uttered a prayer, saying: "By the power of the fast I observe on this *Kamada Ekadashi*, may my husband be freed from his demonic form."

Vashishtha continues: The very moment Lalita spoke these words, the air seemed to shift. A divine light surrounded her husband, and in a miraculous instant, his demonic form vanished. He was restored to his true Gandharva state, radiant and pure once more.

King Yudhishthira, behold the miraculous power of *Kamada Ekadashi*! The husband and wife, now redeemed, took on an even more magnificent form. They ascended to the heavens in a divine chariot, their presence shining brighter than the stars. It was as if the entire universe had conspired to lift them up.

This story reveals the mystical power of *Kamada Ekadashi*. By observing it with full devotion, one can cleanse themselves of sins and earn blessings beyond imagination. O King, even reading or listening to this tale is said to bestow the same rewards as performing the ancient *Vajapeya Yajna* (a sacred Vedic sacrifice believed to bring divine blessings).

Meditation

Visualize standing in a lush garden, beneath a clear blue sky.
A radiant form of Lord Vishnu appears before you, smiling, lotus-eyed, and adorned with yellow silk robes and the Kaustubha jewel.

He speaks silently to your soul:

"Dear one, let go of your past mistakes. You are free. You are loved."

Feel all burdens dissolving in the light of forgiveness and grace.

ॐ Mantra

Sanskrit:

अनिर्देश्यवपुः विष्णुः सर्वसुगतिसुंदरः

Transliteration:

“Anirdeśyavapuḥ Viṣṇuḥ Sarvasugatisaṁdaraḥ”

Meaning:

The form of Vishnu defies words—he is the embodiment of supreme beauty and the giver of all noble destinies.

Chapter 15 — Varuthinī Ekādaśī: The Shield of Virtue 🌿

🏵️ The Day of Divine Protection — Varuthinī Ekādaśī

◆ **English Name:** Varuthini Ekadashi
◆ **Hindi Name:** वरूथिनी एकादशी

◆ **Pronunciation:** *Va-roo-thi-nee Eh-kaa-da-shee*

📅 Tithi and Timing

- **Hindu Calendar Tithi:** Chaitra Krishna Paksha Ekadashi (चैत्र कृष्ण पक्ष एकादशी)

- **Approximate Gregorian Calendar Timing:** April–May

🌙 Astronomical Note:

Varuthinī Ekadashi arises during the waning moon, supporting inner reflection and cleansing of accumulated emotional and karmic residues.

✿ The Sacred Story of Varuthinī Ekādaśī

In ancient times, there lived a mighty and pious king named Mandhata, belonging to the Solar Dynasty. His fame spread across the three worlds for his righteousness and compassion.

Yet, fate plays strangely even with the virtuous.
Once, during a hunting expedition in a dense forest, Mandhata's leg was injured by a wild boar. Though the wound healed externally, his leg became withered and weak, rendering him unable to walk properly.

Distraught and shamed, the noble king abdicated his throne and journeyed deep into the forests, seeking spiritual solace.

In the serene woods, he encountered Sage Vashishta – the seer who had seen countless yugas pass.

Falling humbly at the sage's feet, Mandhata cried:

"O Master of sacred wisdom! My body has failed me,
and my soul is burdened with sorrow.
Is there any path to restoration and salvation?"

Sage Vashishta, his face radiating a serene light, said:

"O virtuous King, your suffering is the ripened fruit of ancient karma.
But despair not!
Soon will come the sacred Varuthinī Ekadashi.
By observing its fast with devotion, you shall be freed from bodily imperfections and attain blessings beyond mortal imagination."

Inspired, King Mandhata rigorously observed the vrata.

On the holy day, he fasted completely, chanted Vishnu's divine names, offered lamps, incense, and fruits, and kept vigil through the night — his heart pouring out in prayer.

On Dwadashi morning, as he completed the fast with gratitude and humility, a brilliant golden radiance engulfed him.

His crippled leg was healed; his body rejuvenated.
His soul soared into states of bliss and divine vision, later attaining the celestial realms — his earthly trials ending in supreme triumph.

Thus, Varuthinī Ekadashi became renowned as the protector of virtues and the healer of past karmic afflictions.

Yudhishthira asked:
"O Vasudeva (a name for Lord Krishna)! What is the name of the Ekadashi (a sacred day of fasting observed every month on the 11th day of the lunar cycle) that falls in the dark fortnight (Krishna Paksha) of the month of Vaishakha? Please describe its glory."

Lord Shri Krishna replied:
"O King! The Ekadashi that falls in the Krishna Paksha (the dark fortnight or waning moon period) of Vaishakha month (according to Gujarat and Maharashtra, this corresponds to Chaitra month) is known by the name 'Varuthini'. It bestows good fortune both in this world and the next. Observing the Vrata (vow) of Varuthini leads to constant happiness and the destruction of sins. Through the observance of this Varuthini Ekadashi, kings like Mandhata and Dhundhumara, and many others, attained the heavenly realms.

The fruit obtained by a human through ten thousand years of penance (spiritual practice) is acquired merely by observing the Varuthini Ekadashi Vrata.

O King! Donating a horse is considered superior to donating an elephant. Greater than that is the donation of land. Even more significant than land donation is the donation of sesame seeds (til-daan). Superior to sesame donation is gold donation (suvarna-daan), and even greater than that is food donation (anna-daan), because the gods, ancestors, and humans are all satisfied by food. Wise sages have equated kanya-daan (the giving away of a daughter in marriage) to these highest forms of donation. Equal in merit to kanya-daan is cow donation (go-daan)—this is the direct assertion of the Lord.

Even beyond all these, the highest merit lies in knowledge donation (vidya-daan). By observing the Varuthini Ekadashi fast, a person attains the fruit equal to that of vidya-daan.

O King! Those who stay awake at night and worship Lord Madhusudana (another name for Lord Vishnu) become free from all sins and attain the supreme destination. Therefore, those who fear sin should devoutly observe this Ekadashi.

One who fears Yamaraja (Lord of Death) must certainly observe the Varuthini Ekadashi Vrata. Merely by reading or hearing about it, a person receives the merit equal to donating a cow ten times (dashagavaan), becomes freed from all sins, and is established in Vishnuloka (the abode of Lord Vishnu)."

Meditation

Visualize a brilliant shield of golden light, spinning gently around your entire being, protecting you from seen and unseen harms.

In the center of this light, Lord Vishnu smiles serenely, holding the Sudarshana Chakra, the conch, the lotus, and the mace — radiating infinite compassion.

ॐ Mantra

Sanskrit:

शरण्यः सर्वभूतानाम्

Transliteration:

"Sharanyah Sarva-bhutanam"

Meaning:

"He who is the protector of all beings."

Chapter 16 — Mohinī Ekādaśī: Liberation from Delusion 🌿

🏵 The Day of Divine Enchantment — Mohinī Ekādaśī

- **English Name:** Mohini Ekadashi
- **Hindi Name:** मोहिनी एकादशी
- **Pronunciation:** *Mo-hi-nee Eh-kaa-da-shee*

📅 Tithi and Timing

- **Hindu Calendar Tithi:** Vaishakha Shukla Paksha Ekadashi (वैशाख शुक्ल पक्ष एकादशी)
- **Approximate Gregorian Calendar Timing:** April–May

🌙 Astronomical Note:

Mohinī Ekadashi occurs during the waxing moon, when inner energies naturally rise, supporting the mind's ability to discriminate truth from illusion.

✿ The Deep Significance of Mohinī Ekādaśī

The name "Mohinī" means "the Enchantress" — referring to the divine form Lord Vishnu took to protect the nectar of immortality (amrita) during the churning of the ocean (Samudra Manthana).

Yet, this Ekadashi is not about succumbing to illusion; it is about being liberated from it. It empowers the devotee to conquer the deepest layers of inner delusion — pride, ignorance, and attachment.

Observing Mohinī Ekadashi grants clarity of perception, strength to overcome Maya (illusion), and unwavering devotion to the Divine.

The Sacred Story of Mohinī Ekādaśī

Yudhishthira asked:
"O Janardana (another name for Lord Krishna, meaning 'liberator of souls')! What is the name of the Ekadashi (the 11th day of the lunar fortnight, considered highly auspicious for fasting and prayer) that falls in the bright half (Shukla Paksha) of the month of Vaishakha

(April–May)? What are its benefits, and what is the method for its observance?"

Lord Shri Krishna replied:
"O Dharmaraja (king of righteousness, referring to Yudhishthira)! In ancient times, the supremely wise Shri Ramachandra (an incarnation of Lord Vishnu and the hero of the epic *Ramayana*) asked this same question to the great sage Vashishtha, which you are now asking me."

Shri Ram said:
"O Lord! I wish to hear about that supreme vrata (religious vow or observance) which destroys all sins and removes all kinds of sorrows."

Sage Vashishtha replied:
"O Shri Ram! You have asked a highly commendable question. Merely uttering your name frees a person from all sins. Still, for the welfare of people, I will describe the supreme vrata among all vratas.

The Ekadashi that falls in the bright fortnight of the month of Vaishakha is known as 'Mohini Ekadashi'. It is extremely virtuous and destroys all sins. By the effect of observing this fast, a person becomes free from the web of illusion (moha) and all sinful tendencies.

On the beautiful banks of the Saraswati river (a sacred river in ancient India), there was a lovely city named Bhadravati. A righteous king named Dyutiman, who belonged to the Chandravansha (the lunar dynasty, one of the two main royal lineages in Hindu tradition) and was known for truthfulness, ruled there. In that same city lived a wealthy and prosperous merchant named Dhanapala. He was always engaged in virtuous deeds. He built rest houses (pyaus – public drinking water stations), wells, monasteries, gardens, ponds, and houses for others. He had deep devotion for Lord Vishnu (the preserver in the Hindu Trinity) and always remained calm.

He had five sons: Sumana, Dyutiman, Meghavi, Sukriti, and Dhrishtha-buddhi. Dhrishtha-buddhi, the fifth son, was constantly engaged in great sinful activities. He was heavily addicted to gambling and other bad habits. He was eager to associate with prostitutes. His intellect neither inclined towards the worship of deities (gods and goddesses) nor towards honoring ancestors (pitras) and Brahmins (priests and scholars of the Vedas). This wicked soul walked the path of injustice and kept wasting his father's wealth.

One day, he was seen wandering at a crossroads with his arm around a prostitute's neck. His father, enraged, threw him out of the house, and his relatives also abandoned him. Now he wandered here and there in misery and grief, bearing one sorrow after another.

One day, due to the influence of some past virtue, he arrived at the ashram (hermitage) of sage Kaudinya. It was the month of Vaishakha, and sage Kaudinya had just returned after bathing in the Ganga (Ganges River, considered the holiest river in Hinduism). Burdened by sorrow, Dhrishtha-buddhi approached the sage, stood before him with folded hands (a gesture of respect in Indian tradition), and said:
"O revered one! O compassionate sage! Kindly have mercy on me and tell me of such a vrata (vow), whose merit can liberate me."

Kaudinya said:
"Observe the vow of Mohini Ekadashi, which falls in the bright fortnight of Vaishakha. By observing fast on Mohini Ekadashi, even the gravest sins accumulated over many births—equivalent in weight to Mount Meru (the mythological golden mountain considered to be the center of all physical, metaphysical, and spiritual universes)—are destroyed."

Sage Vashishtha continued:
"O Shri Ramachandra! Hearing the sage's words, Dhrishtha-buddhi became pleased. Following Kaudinya's instructions, he faithfully observed the Mohini Ekadashi.
O King! By doing so, he became sinless and attained a divine body. Mounted on Garuda (the celestial eagle and vehicle of Lord Vishnu), he ascended to Vaikuntha (Lord Vishnu's divine abode), free from all kinds of worldly afflictions.

Thus, this Mohini Ekadashi vow is supremely beneficial. Simply by reading or listening to its glory, one receives the merit equivalent to donating a thousand cows (considered one of the highest forms of charity in Hinduism)."

Meditation

Imagine yourself in a vast celestial ocean, waves of illusion dancing around you.

At the center, you see the Divine Mohinī – glowing with celestial beauty – scattering the illusions like mist in sunlight.
Focus on the appearance and disappearance of thoughts without attachment. Observe how illusions form and dissolve, realizing their emptiness.

ॐ Mantra

Sanskrit:

मायीनाम् महामायो

Transliteration:

"Māyīnām Mahāmāyo"

Meaning:

"The Supreme Master of Illusion among all beings."

Chapter 17 — Apara Ekādaśī: The Infinite Blessings 🌿

🛕 The Day of Boundless Grace — Apara Ekadashi

- **English Name:** Apara Ekadashi
- **Hindi Name:** अपर एकादशी
- **Pronunciation:** A-*pa-ra Eh-kaa-da-shee*

📅 Tithi and Timing

- **Hindu Calendar Tithi:** Jyeshtha Krishna Paksha Ekadashi (ज्येष्ठ कृष्ण पक्ष एकादशी)
- **Approximate Gregorian Calendar Timing:** May–June

🌙 Astronomical Insight:

Falling during the dark half of Jyeshtha month, Apara Ekadashi aligns with the body's natural tendencies for internal reflection and spiritual detoxification.

Yudhishthira asked:
"O Janardana (a name of Lord Krishna, meaning 'one who helps people'), which Ekadashi falls in the dark fortnight (Krishna Paksha - the waning phase of the moon) of this month? I wish to hear its significance. Please be gracious and tell me."

Lord Shri Krishna replied:
"O King! You have asked a most excellent question for the welfare of all beings. The name of the Ekadashi that occurs in the dark fortnight of this month (according to the regional calendars of Gujarat and Maharashtra, this is the month of Vaishakha - usually April-May) is 'Apara Ekadashi'. It bestows immense religious merit (punya) and destroys even the gravest sins.

Those who give false testimony, cheat in weights and measures, calculate horoscopes and astrology without proper knowledge, or deceitfully practice Ayurveda (an ancient Indian system of medicine) without qualification - such people are believed to dwell in hell (a place of spiritual punishment in the afterlife). However, by observing Apara Ekadashi, even they can become free from sin.

If a Kshatriya (member of the warrior clan) abandons his duty and flees from battle, he incurs severe sin and falls into a dreadful hell. A person who, despite being educated in scriptures, slanders their own Guru (spiritual teacher), also becomes tainted by great sins (mahapataka) and meets a terrible fate. Yet, by observing Apara Ekadashi, even such people can attain spiritual liberation (sadgati).

The spiritual merit (punya) earned by:

- Bathing in the sacred confluence at Prayag (modern-day Prayagraj, India) during the Magha month (January–February) when the sun enters the zodiac sign Capricorn (Makara),
- Observing the festival of Maha Shivaratri (a major Hindu festival dedicated to Lord Shiva) in the city of Kashi (Varanasi),
- Performing pind-daan (ritual offerings for ancestors) at Gaya (Bihar, India) to bring peace to departed souls,
- Bathing in the Godavari River when Jupiter (Brihaspati) is in the sign of Leo (Simha Rashi),
- Visiting the sacred pilgrimage site Badrinath and having darshan (sacred

viewing) of Lord Kedarnath (a form of Lord Shiva) (In Uttarakhand, India),

- Or performing a yajna (Vedic sacrificial ritual) at Kurukshetra (Haryana, India) during a solar eclipse, along with charitable donations of elephants, horses, and gold –

All this merit is said to be equaled by observing Apara Ekadashi.

By fasting on this day and worshipping Lord Vamana (a dwarf incarnation of Lord Vishnu), one becomes free from all sins and attains Vaikuntha (the eternal abode of Lord Vishnu).

✿ Meditation

"*Sit quietly.*
Imagine a pure river of golden light descending from the heavens.
Visualize yourself placing all your past burdens into this river — mistakes, regrets, fears — watching them dissolve into light."

Feel lighter, freer — embraced by Lord Vishnu's endless mercy.

Mantras

Sanskrit:

अनन्तम् अव्ययम् क्षान्तम्

Transliteration:

"Anantam avyayam kshantam"

Meaning:

Infinite, Immutable, the Embodiment of Forgiveness.

Chapter 18 — Nirjala Ekādaśī: The Supreme Fast

The Day of Supreme Renunciation — Nirjala Ekadashi

- **English Name:** Nirjala Ekadashi
- **Hindi Name:** निर्जला एकादशी
- **Pronunciation:** *Nir-ja-la Eh-kaa-da-shee*

Tithi and Timing

- **Hindu Calendar Tithi:** Jyeshtha Shukla Paksha Ekadashi (ज्येष्ठ शुक्ल पक्ष एकादशी)
- **Approximate Gregorian Calendar Timing:** May–June

Astronomical Insight:

During the bright half of Jyeshtha, fasting completely **without food or even water** (Nirjala) aligns the body's inner fire (Agni) to its highest spiritual clarity.

The Divine Story of Nirjala Ekādaśī

Yudhishthira said:
"O Janardana (another name for Lord Krishna, meaning 'one who helps all beings'), please describe the Ekadashi that falls in the bright fortnight (Shukla Paksha) of the month of Jyeshtha (a Hindu month falling around May-June)."

Lord Shri Krishna replied:
"O King! That description will be given by the highly righteous son of Satyavati, Sage Vyasa (the compiler of the Vedas and author of the Mahabharata), as he is thoroughly learned in all scriptures and the Vedas along with their branches."

Then Sage Vyasa spoke:
"One should not eat food on the day of Ekadashi, whether it falls in the bright or dark fortnight. On Ekadashi, after bathing and purifying oneself, one should worship Lord Keshava (a name of Lord Vishnu) with flowers. After completing daily duties, one must first serve food to Brahmins (the priestly class in Hindu tradition) and only then eat.
O King! Even during impurity caused by birth or death in the family (Janmaashauch or Maranaashauch), food should not be taken on Ekadashi."

Bhimasena said:
"O supremely intelligent grandfather! Please listen to me. King Yudhishthira, Mother Kunti, Draupadi, Arjuna, Nakula, and Sahadeva never eat on Ekadashi and always tell me:
'Bhimasena! You too should not eat on Ekadashi.'
But I say to them: 'I cannot bear hunger.'"

Sage Vyasa said:
"If you desire to attain Svargaloka (the celestial heaven) and consider Naraka (hell) undesirable, then you must avoid food on both Ekadashis each month."

Bhima replied:
"O supremely wise grandfather! I speak the truth before you. Even eating once a day is difficult for me—how can I fast?
In my stomach burns a fire called Vrika (a mythical fire likened to the hunger of a wolf), which is pacified only when I eat heavily.
Therefore, O great sage, I can only fast once a year. Please suggest a single fast that yields the benefits of all Ekadashis and brings spiritual welfare. I will follow it properly."

Sage Vyasa replied:
"Bhima! During the month of Jyeshtha, when the Sun is in Taurus (Vrishabha Rashi) or Gemini (Mithuna Rashi), observe the bright

fortnight's Ekadashi with full discipline as Nirjala Ekadashi (Ekadashi observed without water).
You may only put water in your mouth for rinsing or ritual sipping (achaman), but no other form of water or food should be consumed.
From sunrise on Ekadashi until sunrise the next day (Dwadashi), one must abstain from water completely for the vow to be complete.
By observing Nirjala Ekadashi, one earns the merit (punya) of observing all 24 Ekadashis of the year—this is certain."

Sage Vyasa continued:
"Lord Keshava (Vishnu, the protector deity in the Hindu Trinity) once told me: 'If a person surrenders only to Me and remains fasting on Ekadashi, he is freed from all sins.'
Fearsome messengers of Yama (the god of death and justice), with dreadful forms and dark complexions, do not approach those who observe Nirjala Ekadashi.
Instead, the messengers of Vishnu (Vishnudutas), who wear yellow garments (pitambar), hold the divine discus (Sudarshan Chakra), and move as fast as thought, come at death and take the soul to the divine abode of Lord Vishnu."

Vyasa said further:
"Therefore, observe Nirjala Ekadashi with devotion and worship Shri Hari (another name of Vishnu).
Even if someone has committed sins as vast as Mount Meru (the mythological sacred mountain), those sins are destroyed by observing this fast.
On this day, following the vow of abstaining from water (nirjala) gives the same merit as donating millions of gold coins every hour.
Any action done on this day—be it bathing, charity, chanting, or fire rituals—is eternal (akshaya). This is Lord Krishna's own declaration.

"Those who fast and give charity on Jyeshtha Shukla Ekadashi attain the supreme goal (parama pada).

Vyasa then instructed:
"O son of Kunti! Listen to the special gifts and duties for pious men and women on Nirjala Ekadashi:
Worship Lord Vishnu, who rests upon the cosmic ocean (Kshira Sagara), and donate a pot of water (Udakumbha), or a symbolic water cow (Jala-Dhenu), or an actual cow or ghee-cow (cow made from clarified butter used ritually).

With sufficient monetary offerings (dakshina) and varieties of food, satisfy the Brahmins. When they are pleased, Lord Hari grants liberation (moksha).
Whoever, with self-control (shama and dama), worships Vishnu, stays awake all night (jagaran), and observes Nirjala Ekadashi, uplifts not just themselves but also their past 100 and future 100 generations to the abode of Lord Vasudeva (another name for Vishnu)."

"On this day, one should donate food, clothes, cows, water, beds (shayya), fine seating (asana), water pots (kamandalu), and umbrellas.
Whoever donates shoes to a worthy Brahmin attains a place in heaven riding a golden chariot (vimana).
Whoever listens to or narrates the glory of Nirjala Ekadashi sincerely will go to Svargaloka (the heavenly realm).
The merit gained by bathing during a solar eclipse or on new moon (Amavasya) is equal to merely hearing about this Ekadashi."

"Before sunrise, one should brush their teeth and resolve (sankalpa):
'I will remain without food or water (except for ritual sipping) on this Ekadashi for the pleasure of Lord Keshava (Vishnu).'

One should worship Lord Vishnu with fragrance (gandha), incense (dhupa), flowers (pushpa), and fine clothes (vastra), and while offering a pot of water as charity, recite the following mantra:

Mantra:
Devadeva Hrishikesha! Samsararnava Taraka, Udakumbha Dānena, Nay Maam Paramaam Gatim.
(O Lord of Lords, Hrishikesha—controller of senses—who helps cross the ocean of worldly life, by the donation of this water pot, please grant me the supreme state.)

Vyasa concluded:
"O Bhimasena! On the bright Ekadashi of Jyeshtha, observe the Nirjala vow, and donate water pots with sugar to worthy Brahmins.
By doing this, one reaches near Lord Vishnu and experiences divine joy.
On the next day (Dwadashi), after feeding Brahmins, one may eat.
One who completely observes this sin-destroying Ekadashi becomes free of all sins and attains a joyful spiritual state."

After hearing this, Bhimasena began to observe this sacred fast, and from that time onward, this Ekadashi became famous in the world as Pandava Ekadashi (named after the

Pandavas of the Mahabharata).

✿ Meditation

"Close your eyes.
Visualize a brilliant flame within your heart – flickering, steady, pure.
Feel your hungers, your thirsts, your desires – all offered into this inner yajna (sacred fire).
As the flame consumes all cravings, imagine your soul soaring upward – light, free, eternal."

✿ Mantras

Sanskrit:

शान्ताकारं भुजगशयनं पद्मनाभं सुरेशं
विश्वाधारं गगनसदृशं मेघवर्णं शुभाङ्गम्।
लक्ष्मीकान्तं कमलनयनं योगिभिर्ध्यानगम्यम्
वन्दे विष्णुं भवभयहरं सर्वलोकैकनाथम्॥

Transliteration:

Śāntākāraṁ bhujagaśayanaṁ padmanābhaṁ sureśaṁ
Viśvādhāraṁ gaganasadṛśaṁ meghavarṇaṁ śubhāṅgam।
Lakṣmīkāntaṁ kamalanayanaṁ yogibhir-dhyānagamyam

Vande viṣṇuṁ bhavabhayaharaṁ
sarvalokaikanāthamǁ

Meaning:

"I bow to Lord Vishnu who has a peaceful appearance, who reclines on the serpent (Shesha Naag), who has a lotus in his navel, who is the lord of the gods, who is the support of the universe, who is boundless like the sky, who has the color of clouds, who has a beautiful form, who is the consort of Lakshmi, who has lotus-like eyes, who is attainable through meditation by yogis, who is the remover of the fear of worldly existence, and who is the Lord of all worlds."

Chapter 19 – Yogini Ekādaśī: Healing of the Soul

The Day of Soul Healing — Yogini Ekadashi

- **English Name:** Yogini Ekadashi
- **Hindi Name:** योगिनी एकादशी
- **Pronunciation:** *Yo-gi-ni Eh-kaa-da-shee*

Tithi and Timing

- **Hindu Calendar Tithi:** Ashadha Krishna Paksha Ekadashi (आषाढ़ कृष्ण पक्ष एकादशी)
- **Approximate Gregorian Calendar Timing:** June–July

Astronomical Insight:

During the dark fortnight of Ashadha, Yogini Ekadashi arrives as a healing tide, helping the mind shed old burdens, much like the moon relinquishes her light.

Story of Yogini Ekādaśī

Yudhishthira asked: O *Vasudeva (another name for Lord Krishna, a central deity in Hinduism)! What is the name of the Ekadashi that falls in the Krishna Paksha (the dark fortnight or waning phase of the moon) of the month of* Ashadha *(roughly June–July in the Gregorian calendar)? Please describe it in detail.*

Lord Shri Krishna said: O *King! The Ekadashi that falls in the Krishna Paksha of the month of* Ashadha *(according to the calendar followed in* Gujarat *and* Maharashtra*—states in western* India*) is called* "Yogini"*. It is a destroyer of great sins and acts like an eternal boat (a spiritual metaphor for salvation or deliverance) for beings drowning in the ocean of worldly existence (referring to the cycle of birth, death, and rebirth, known as samsara).*

The king of Alakapuri *(a mythical city said to be the abode of* Kubera*, the god of wealth),* Kubera*, was always devoted to the worship of* Lord Shiva *(a major deity in* Hinduism*, often associated with destruction and transformation). He had a* Yaksha *(a nature-spirit or demigod in* Hindu *mythology, usually associated with wealth and service to deities) servant named* "Hemamali" *who used to bring* *flowers for the worship. Hemamali's wife was named "Vishalakshi" (meaning "broad-eyed," a name associated with feminine beauty and auspiciousness). Ensnared by the bonds of lust (referred to as kama, or sensual desire), this Yaksha remained constantly attached to his wife. One day, Hemamali brought flowers from Manasarovara (a sacred lake near Mount Kailash in Tibet, considered holy in Hinduism, Buddhism, and Jainism) but stayed back at home, engrossed in the pleasures with his wife, and did not go to Kubera's palace.*

Meanwhile, Kubera was sitting in the temple and waiting to worship Lord Shiva. He waited till noon for the flowers to arrive. When the time for worship (called puja, a ritualistic offering to a deity) passed and the flowers still hadn't come, Kubera, in anger, asked his attendants: "O Yakshas! Why hasn't the wicked Hemamali arrived yet?"

The Yakshas replied: "O King! He is indulging in sensual pleasures at home with his wife, overwhelmed by lust." Hearing this, Kubera became filled with rage and immediately summoned Hemamali. Hemamali came and stood before Kubera. Seeing him, Kubera spoke: "O sinner! O wicked one! O immoral! You have shown disrespect toward the Lord. Therefore, be afflicted with leprosy, be separated from your beloved wife, and fall from this place (meaning he is banished from the celestial or divine realm). Go to some other realm."

Upon Kubera's words, Hemamali fell from that place. His entire body was afflicted with leprosy, yet due to the merit of Shiva worship, his power of remembrance (smaran-shakti, the spiritual ability to remember sacred truths) did not diminish. Thereafter, he went to the peaks of Mount Meru (a sacred mountain). There, he had the darshan (a vision or sighting of a divine or holy person, believed to confer blessings) of the sage Markandeya (an immortal sage in Hinduism, known for his deep wisdom and long life). The sin-ridden Yaksha offered prostration (a gesture of respect and submission) at the sage's feet. Sage Markandeya saw him trembling with fear and asked: "How have you come to be afflicted with leprosy?"

The Yaksha said: "O Sage! I am Hemamali, an attendant of Kubera. I used to bring flowers from Manasarovara every day and offer them to Kubera for Lord Shiva's worship. One day, caught in the pleasure of union with my wife, I lost sense of time. King Kubera, in his anger, cursed me—so I became afflicted with leprosy and was separated from my beloved. O Sage!

Knowing that saints are naturally inclined toward compassion, please instruct this sinner in a way of atonement (a spiritual act of penance or correction)."

Sage Markandeya said: *You have spoken the truth here; therefore, I shall instruct you in a path of welfare. Observe the vrata (a religious vow or fast) of the "Yogini Ekadashi" which falls in the Krishna Paksha of the month of Ashadha. By the merit of this vrata, your leprosy will certainly be cured.*

Lord Shri Krishna continued: O *King! By the instruction of Sage Markandeya, Hemamali observed the Yogini Ekadashi vrata, by which his body was completely freed from leprosy. By performing that great vrata, he became fully happy once again.*

O *King! The vrata of "Yogini" is so meritorious that the same result which one obtains by feeding eighty-eight thousand Brahmins (priests and learned scholars in Hindu tradition, often offered food in religious charity) is obtained by a human who observes the Yogini Ekadashi. "Yogini" destroys great sins and bestows great merits. By reading and hearing this glory (mahatmya, a spiritual tale that conveys the greatness of a deity, holy day, or ritual), one becomes free from all sins.*

✿ Meditation

"Visualize yourself as a lotus bud submerged in muddy waters.
As you breathe slowly, imagine the petals unfolding – one by one – lifting you upward, beyond pain, sorrow, and regret.
Feel yourself blossoming in the light of Vishnu's infinite compassion."

✿ Mantras

Sanskrit:

सर्वगतः श्रीविभावनः

Transliteration:

Sarvagataḥ Śrīvibhāvanaḥ

Meaning:

The all-pervading Lord who spreads divine prosperity everywhere.

Chapter 20 – Devshayani Ekādaśī: Lord's Divine Slumber 🌿

🛕 The Day of Cosmic Rest — Devshayani Ekadashi

- **English Name:** Devshayani Ekadashi
- **Hindi Name:** देवशयनी एकादशी
- **Pronunciation:** *De-va-sha-ya-nee Eh-kaa-da-shee*

📅 Tithi and Timing

- **Hindu Calendar Tithi:** Ashadha Shukla Paksha Ekadashi (आषाढ़ शुक्ल पक्ष एकादशी)
- **Approximate Gregorian Calendar Timing:** June–July

🌙 Astronomical Insight:

Devshayani Ekadashi coincides with the arrival of Dakshinayana (the Sun's southward journey), symbolizing inward retreat, deeper contemplation, and spiritual hibernation.

✿ The Cosmic Silence of Devshayani Ekādaśī

On this sacred day, Lord Vishnu enters divine sleep (Yoga Nidra) upon the cosmic ocean, resting on the serpent Ananta Shesha.

It is a mystical period where the deities rest, and human beings are invited to awaken their own inner divinity.

Thus, Devshayani Ekadashi marks the beginning of Chaturmasya — the holy four months of penance, simplicity, and heightened devotion.

The Lord rests outwardly, but becomes more accessible inwardly to the seekers who call out to Him.

Story of Devshayani Ekādaśī

Yudhishthira asked: O *Bhagavan (Lord), which Ekadashi falls in the Shukla Paksha (bright fortnight or waxing phase of the moon) of the month of Ashadha (June–July)? Please be kind enough to tell me its name and procedure (vidhi).*

Lord Shri Krishna said: O *King! The Ekadashi that falls in the Shukla Paksha of Ashadha is called Shayani Ekadashi. I shall now describe it. It is extremely meritorious (maha-punyamayi), grants svarga (heaven) and moksha (liberation), removes all sins (sarva-papahara), and is the supreme vrata (sacred observance).*

On the day of Shayani Ekadashi in the Shukla Paksha of Ashadha, those who worship Lord Vishnu—Kamala-lochana (lotus-eyed)—with lotus flowers and observe the Ekadashi vrata properly, have effectively worshipped the three worlds and the three eternal deities (Brahma, Vishnu, Shiva).

On the day of Hari-Shayani Ekadashi, one form of Mine resides with King Bali, and another lies asleep upon the serpent bed (Shesha Shaiyya) in the Kshira Sagara (Ocean of Milk), until the arrival of Kartika Shukla Ekadashi (four months later).

Therefore, from Ashadha Shukla Ekadashi to Kartika Shukla Ekadashi, a person should conduct themselves with strict observance of dharma (righteousness).

Whoever observes this vrata attains the supreme state (param gati); thus, this Ekadashi should be followed with utmost devotion. On the night of Ekadashi, one should remain awake in vigil (jagaran) and worship Lord Vishnu, who bears the conch (shankha), discus (chakra), and mace (gada) with complete devotion.

Even Brahma, the four-headed creator, cannot measure the merit (punya) earned by such a person.

Those who spend the Chaturmasya period (the four holy months from Ashadha to Kartika) performing deep-dana (lamp offerings), eating meals on palasha leaves (Butea monosperma), and observing vratas, are truly My beloved.

During Chaturmasya, Lord Vishnu is said to be asleep, so humans should also sleep on the ground in humility. One should avoid certain foods as a mark of self-restraint: in Shravana (July–August) avoid leafy vegetables (saag); in Bhadrapada (August–September) avoid curd (yogurt); in Ashwin (September–October) avoid milk; and in Kartika (October–November) avoid pulses (dal).

Whoever follows brahmacharya (celibacy or spiritual discipline) during Chaturmasya attains the highest spiritual goal (param gati).

O King! Through the vrata of Ekadashi alone, a person is freed from all sins. Therefore, one should always observe it and never forget it.

Among the Ekadashis that fall between Shayani Ekadashi and Bodhini Ekadashi (the day when Lord Vishnu is said to awaken), only those that fall in the Krishna Paksha (dark fortnight) are suitable for grihasthas (householders); the Krishna Paksha Ekadashis of other months are not considered appropriate for householders.

However, all Shukla Paksha Ekadashis (bright fortnight) should be observed by everyone.

✿ Meditation

"Visualize yourself floating effortlessly upon a vast, serene ocean.
The waves rise and fall, yet your true Self remains unmoved beneath them.
Feel the rhythmic breathing of the universe merge with your own."

✿ Mantra

Sanskrit: पद्मनाभः

Transliteration: *Padmanābhaḥ*
Meaning: *"The Lord from whose navel springs the lotus of creation."*

Chapter 21 – Kamika Ekādaśī: Blossoming of Inner Bhakti 🌿

🛕 The Day of Divine Flowering — Kamika Ekadashi

- **English Name:** Kamika Ekadashi
- **Hindi Name:** कामिका एकादशी
- **Pronunciation:** *Kaa-mee-kaa Eh-kaa-da-shee*

📅 Tithi and Timing

- **Hindu Calendar Tithi:** Shravana Krishna Paksha Ekadashi (श्रावण कृष्ण पक्ष एकादशी)
- **Approximate Gregorian Calendar Timing:** July–August

🌙 Astronomical Insight:

During the rains of Shravana, the Earth blooms anew – similarly, Kamika Ekadashi inspires the blooming of devotion in the inner heart.

✿ Story of Kamika Ekādaśī

Yudhishthira asked: *Govinda! Vasudeva!* I offer my salutations to you. Please tell me: Which Ekadashi falls in the Krishna Paksha (*the waning phase of the moon*) of the month of Shravana (*July–August in the Hindu lunar calendar; sometimes called Ashadha in Gujarat and Maharashtra*)? Kindly describe it in detail.

Lord Shri Krishna replied: O King, listen carefully. I shall narrate to you a sin-destroying story that Sage Bhrigu once told to Sage Narada upon being asked a similar question.

Narada had asked: O *Bhagavan* (*a reverent term for the Supreme Lord*), O *Kamalāsana* (*"one seated on a lotus," referring to Lord Brahma, the creator deity who is depicted as seated on a lotus flower*), I wish to hear from you about the Ekadashi (*11th lunar day*) that falls in the Krishna Paksha of Shravana. What is its name? Who is the presiding deity? And what merit does it bestow?

Bhrigu replied: Narada, listen! Desiring the welfare of all the worlds, I will now answer your question. The Ekadashi that falls in the Krishna Paksha of the month of Shravana is called Kamika Ekadashi. Merely remembering it bestows the merit of performing a Vajapeya Yajna (*an elaborate and ancient Vedic fire ritual typically performed by kings or sages for great spiritual and worldly rewards*).

On this day, one should worship the Lord using names like:

- Shridhar (*Bearer of fortune*),
- Hari (*Remover of sins*),
- Vishnu (*All-pervading One*),
- Madhava (*Consort of Goddess Lakshmi*),
- and Madhusudana (*Slayer of the demon Madhu*).

The merit gained from worshipping Lord Shri Krishna on this day surpasses even the merit one gains from visiting India's most sacred places:

- Ganga (*the holy River Ganges*),
- Kashi (*the ancient city of Varanasi*),
- Naimisharanya (*a sacred forest mentioned in scriptures*),
- and Pushkara Kshetra (*a holy town with one of the few temples to Lord Brahma*).

Even bathing in the Godavari River (*another revered river in India*) during rare and auspicious astrological alignments—such as:

- Simha Rashi's Guru (*Jupiter in the zodiac sign* Leo),
- Vyatipata and Danda Yoga (*powerful cosmic combinations in* Vedic *astrology*)—

does not offer the spiritual benefit that comes from worshipping Lord Krishna on Kamika Ekadashi.

One who donates the entire earth filled with forests and oceans is considered equal in merit to someone who observes the Kamika Ekadashi vrata.

Even donating a cow with all auspicious accessories (*such as ornaments, cloth, or calf*), traditionally regarded as an act of immense charity, bestows the same spiritual merit as observing Kamika Ekadashi.

O King! Worshipping Lord Shridhar during Shravana month is believed to spiritually satisfy not just the deity himself, but also:

- Gandharvas (*celestial musicians*),
- Nagas (*serpent-like semi-divine beings*),

- and the entire host of Devas (*divine beings or gods*).

Thus, those who are fearful of accumulating sin (bad karma) should worship Shri Hari (*a name of Lord Vishnu*) according to their capacity on Kamika Ekadashi. It is especially recommended for people lost in the *ocean of worldly life*—described metaphorically as being stuck in the *mud of sin*.

Even compared to those who are deeply established in spiritual disciplines, a person who observes Kamika Ekadashi vrata achieves even greater spiritual fruit.

One who stays awake at night (Jagaran) on this day in prayer and worship never encounters the terrifying Yama-dutas (*messengers of Yama, the god of death*), nor do they fall into bad destinies in the afterlife.

Even though one might worship Lord Vishnu with costly offerings like rubies, pearls, cat's eye gems (vaidurya), and coral, He is more pleased when offered a simple Tulsi leaf (*holy basil, sacred to Vishnu*).

He who offers Tulsi manjari (*flowering tops of the Tulsi plant*) to Shri Keshava (*another name of Vishnu*) is freed from all sins committed during his lifetime.

Tulsi Stotra (Hymn in Praise of Tulsi)

Sanskrit:

या दृष्टा निखिलाघसङ्घशमनी स्पृष्टा वपुःपावनी
रोगाणामभिवन्दिता निरसनी सृष्ट्यन्तकद्राविणी ।
प्रात्यस्मृतिविधायिनी भगवतः कृष्णस्य संरोपिता
न्यस्ता तच्चरणे विमुक्तिफलदा तस्यै तुलस्यै नमः ॥

Transliteration:

yā dṛṣṭā nikhilāghasaṅghaśamanī spṛṣṭā vapuḥpāvanī
rogāṇām abhivanditā nirasanī sṛṣṭyantakadrāviṇī |
prātyasmṛtividhāyinī bhagavataḥ kṛṣṇasya saṁropitā
nyastā taccaraṇe vimuktiphaladā tasyai tulasyai namaḥ ||

Translation:

"She who destroys all accumulated sins merely by being seen,
Who purifies the body when touched,
Who removes diseases when worshipped,
And when watered, causes even Yama (*the god of death*) to tremble—
She who, when planted, brings one close to Lord Krishna,
And when offered at His feet, grants liberation (moksha)—

To that Tulsi Devi, I offer my respectful salutations."

A person who performs Deep-dan (*the offering of lighted lamps*) during Ekadashi—both during the day and at night—acquires such immense spiritual merit that even Chitragupta (*the divine accountant who keeps records of karma*) cannot calculate it.

Lighting even a single lamp of ghee (clarified butter) or til oil (sesame oil) in front of Lord Krishna on this day causes one's ancestors to enjoy amrit (nectar of immortality) in Swarga-loka (heaven).

After death, such a person ascends to heaven, where they are honored and worshipped with millions of divine lamps as a result of their Ekadashi offering.

Lord Krishna said: O Yudhishthira! Thus, I have described to you the glories of Kamika Ekadashi. It is the destroyer of all sins and the grantor of heaven (svarga) and great merit.

Therefore, all human beings should certainly observe this vrata (sacred vow).
He who listens to this Mahatmya (*glorious narration or spiritual account*) with devotion is freed from all sins and attains the eternal abode of Lord Vishnu—Vaikuntha (*a blissful*

spiritual realm beyond the material world).

✿ Meditation

*"Close your eyes and visualize a radiant lotus blooming within your heart.
In the center of this lotus sits Lord Vishnu, serene and smiling.
Feel your every breath as an offering at His feet."*

✿ Mantra

Sanskrit: हृषीकेशः

Transliteration: Hṛṣīkeśaḥ

Meaning: *"The Lord of the Senses – He who commands all inner and outer movements."*

Chapter 22 — Pavitropana Ekādaśī (Putrada Ekādaśī): The Thread of Purity 🌿

🛕 The Sacred Day of Spiritual Cleansing — Pavitropana Ekadashi

- **English Name:** Pavitropana Ekadashi
- **Hindi Name:** पवित्रोपना एकादशी
- **Pronunciation:** *Puh-vi-tro-pa-na Eh-kaa-da-shee*
- **Alternate Name:** Putrada Ekādaśī (2nd)

📅 Tithi and Timing

- **Hindu Calendar Tithi:** Shravana Shukla Paksha Ekadashi (श्रावण शुक्ल पक्ष एकादशी)
- **Approximate Gregorian Calendar Timing:** August

🌙 Astronomical Insight:

During the waxing phase of the moon in Shravana, the energies of renewal and purification are most potent.

✿ Story of Pavitropana (Putrada) Ekādaśī

Yudhishthira asked: "O Madhusudana (a name for Lord Krishna), what is the name of the Ekadashi that falls in the Shukla Paksha (the bright fortnight, the first half of the lunar month) of the month of Shravan (a month in the Hindu calendar, typically falling around July-August)? Please describe it to me in detail."

Bhagavan Shri Krishna replied:
"O King! This is an ancient tale from the beginning of the Dvapara Yuga (one of the four ages in Hindu cosmology). In a city called Mahishmati (an ancient city in India), there was a king named Mahijit who ruled his kingdom righteously. However, he had no son, and therefore, the kingdom did not bring him any real happiness. Seeing his condition, the king became deeply worried. He sat in the assembly of priests and said:

O revered Brahmins (learned scholars and priests)! I have committed no sin in this life. I have not accumulated wealth unjustly in my treasury. I have never taken wealth belonging to Brahmins or the gods. I have followed the prescribed rituals and duties of a householder (a person who fulfills family and social responsibilities). I have conquered the earth by following Dharma (righteousness, moral law). I have punished the wicked, even if they were like my own kin or sons. I have always respected learned and virtuous men, and have never shown contempt for anyone. Then why is it that I have not been blessed with a son? Please think about this matter.

Hearing the king's words, the priests and Brahmins, concerned for his welfare, entered a dense forest in search of a solution. They began wandering in search of a sage (a wise and spiritually advanced person) who was devoted to penance (spiritual discipline). Eventually, they came upon the great sage Lomasha.

Lomasha was a knower of Dharma (righteousness), master of all scriptures, long-lived, and a great soul. His body was covered in hair, and he radiated the same brilliance as Lord Brahma (the creator deity in Hinduism). It is said that with the passing of each Kalpa (cosmic cycle, about 4.32 billion human years), one hair on his body falls off — hence, he is known as Lomasha. This great sage knew the past, present, and future.

Seeing the people approaching, Lomasha Muni (sage Lomasha) asked, Why have you come here? Tell me the reason for your arrival. Whatever is beneficial for you, I shall certainly do.

The Brahmins said, O sage! There is a king named Mahijit, who has no son. We are his priests, and he has treated us like his own sons. Seeing his sorrow, we have come here with firm resolve to perform penance. O great sage! By the fortune of the king, we have now been blessed with your darshan (sacred sight of a holy person). Just seeing a great soul fulfills all desires. Please instruct us in a method by which the king may obtain a son.

Hearing this, Sage Lomasha entered into deep meditation for a short time. Then, having come to know the account of the king's previous life, he said:

O priests! Listen. In his previous life, King Mahijit was a poor and greedy merchant (someone who buys and sells goods for profit). He traveled from village to village to conduct his trade. One day, during the Shukla Paksha of the month of Jyeshtha (the bright fortnight of the month of May-June), on the tenth day (Dashami), when the sun was scorching at midday, he came to a reservoir (a place with a large amount of water, like a pond or lake) on the outskirts of a village. Seeing a well filled with water, he went to drink. Just then, a cow arrived there with her calf (a young cow). Parched with thirst and exhausted by the heat, the cow entered the well to drink. But the merchant drove her away and drank the water himself. Because of this sinful act (a morally wrong act), he has now been born without a son. Due to some merits (good deeds) from another birth, he has obtained a peaceful and obstacle-free kingdom.

The priests said, O sage! It is said in the Puranas (ancient Hindu scriptures) that sinful acts are destroyed by virtuous deeds. Please instruct us in such a righteous act that will destroy the sin from his past.

Lomasha Muni replied, O priests! The Ekadashi that falls during the Shukla Paksha of the month of Shravan is known as Putrada Ekadashi. It is famed for granting the desire of progeny (children). All of you should observe the vrata (a vow or religious observance) of that Ekadashi.

Hearing this, the priests offered obeisance (respectful salutation) to the sage and returned to the city. There, they faithfully observed the Putrada Ekadashi vrata, keeping vigil through the night and offering its pure merit to the king. Thereafter, the queen conceived, and in due course, gave birth to a powerful son.

By hearing the glory of this Ekadashi, one is freed from all sins, enjoys happiness in this world, and attains a divine destination in the next.

✿ Meditation

"Visualize a silken, radiant thread descending from the crown of your head, linking you directly to the lotus feet of Lord Vishnu. Feel this golden connection dissolving all impurities, leaving only pure, vibrant light."

✿ Mantra

Sanskrit: ॐ पवित्रात्मने नमः

Transliteration: "Om Pavitratmane Namah"

Meaning: Salutations to the One who is the very embodiment of Purity.

Chapter 23 — Aja Ekādaśī: Release from Past Burdens 🌿

🛕 The Sacred Day of Inner Liberation — Aja Ekadashi

- **English Name:** Aja Ekadashi
- **Hindi Name:** अजा एकादशी
- **Pronunciation:** A-*juh Eh-kaa-da-shee*

📅 Tithi and Timing

- **Hindu Calendar Tithi:** Bhādrapada Krishna Paksha Ekadashi (भाद्रपद कृष्ण पक्ष एकादशी)
- **Approximate Gregorian Calendar Timing:** August–September

🌙 Astronomical Insight:

Falling during the waning phase of Bhādrapada, Aja Ekadashi supports deep karmic cleansing and emotional healing.

✿ The Story of Aja Ekādaśī

Yudhishthira asked:
"O Janardana (a name of Lord Krishna, meaning 'Savior of people')!

Now I wish to know which Ekadashi falls in the Krishna Paksha (*the waning phase of the moon*) of the month of Bhadrapada (August–*September in the Hindu lunar calendar; sometimes called Shravan in Gujarat and Maharashtra*)? Kindly describe it in detail.

Lord Shri Krishna replied:
"O King! Listen with full attention. The name of the Ekadashi that falls in the Krishna Paksha of the Bhadrapada month is *Aja Ekadashi*. It is said to destroy all sins. One who observes this fast with worship of Lord Hrishikesha (another name for Krishna, meaning 'Lord of the senses') becomes free from all sins.

In ancient times, there was a renowned king named *Harishchandra* (a legendary king in Hindu lore known for his unwavering truthfulness), who was the sovereign of the entire earth and always spoke the truth. Once, due to the result of a past karma (deed or action that causes future consequences), he lost his kingdom. The king had to sell his wife and son. Then, he even sold himself. Though he was a pious soul, he was forced to become a servant of a *Chandala* (a member of a caste, often associated with handling the dead). He used to collect shrouds (funeral cloths) from corpses. Even then, King Harishchandra did not deviate from truth.

In this manner, many years passed while he served the Chandala. The king became deeply troubled. Greatly sorrowed, he thought: 'What should I do? Where should I go? How will I attain deliverance?' Thinking thus, he became immersed in an ocean of grief.

Seeing the king immersed in sorrow, the great sage *Gautama* (an ancient revered Hindu sage or rishi) came to him. Seeing the revered Brahmin (member of the priestly class in Hindu society) arrive, the king bowed at his feet, folded his hands, and stood before Gautama, narrating his entire sorrowful story.

Hearing the king's words, Sage Gautama said: O King! In the Krishna Paksha of the Bhadrapada month, an extremely auspicious Ekadashi named *Aja* is approaching. It bestows great merit. Observe its fast — it will put an end to your sins. By your good fortune, the Ekadashi falls on the seventh day from today. On that day, observe a fast and remain awake throughout the night (a common practice called *jagaran*, signifying spiritual vigilance).

Saying this, Sage Gautama disappeared (a common motif symbolizing divine sages appearing and vanishing after delivering wisdom).

Hearing the sage's words, King Harishchandra observed that supreme fast (vrata – a vow of fasting and spiritual observance) of Aja Ekadashi. By the power of that *vrata*, the king overcame all his sufferings. He was reunited with his wife, and his son regained his life. Celestial drums resounded in the sky, and flowers rained down from the heavens (symbolizing divine approval and joy).

By the influence of Ekadashi, the king regained an unobstructed kingdom and finally, along with his citizens and relatives, attained the heavenly abode (*Svargalok* – the celestial heaven in Hindu belief).

O King Yudhishthira! Whoever observes this fast becomes free from all sins and ascends to the heavenly realms. Simply reading or listening to this story yields the merit equivalent to performing an *Ashwamedha Yajna* (a highly sacred and royal Vedic horse-sacrifice ritual symbolizing absolute sovereignty and great religious merit)."

Meditation

"Visualize all burdens – regrets, mistakes, sorrows – as dry leaves around you. Imagine the brilliant light of Lord Vishnu descending and gently burning them away, leaving you light, pure, and free."

Mantra

Sanskrit:

ॐ कर्मविमोचकाय नमः

Transliteration:

"Om Karmavimochakaya Namah"

Meaning:

Meaning: "Salutations to the One who liberates from karma.

Chapter 24 — Padha Ekadashi: The Divine Turn on Lord Hari's Serpent Bed

The Sacred Day of Spiritual Growth — Padha Ekadashi

- **English Name**: Padha Ekadashi
- **Hindi Name**: पधा एकादशी
- **Pronunciation**: Pad-hā Ekaadashi

Tithi and Timing

• **Hindu Calendar Tithi**: Bhadrapada Shukla Paksha Ekadashi (भाद्रपद शुक्ल पक्ष एकादशी)

• **Approximate Gregorian Calendar Timing**: August–September

Astronomical Note

As the moon waxes towards fullness in Bhadrapada, the energy amplifies intentions and spiritual resolutions.

ॐ The Story of Padhā Ekadashi

Yudhishthira (the eldest of the five Pandava brothers and a righteous king in the Mahabharata) once asked Lord Krishna:

"O Keshava (another name of Lord Krishna)! Please tell me the name of the that falls in the bright fortnight (Shukla Paksha) of the month of Bhadrapada (August–September). Who is the presiding deity of that day, and what is the proper way to observe it?"

Shri Krishna replied:

"O King! Listen carefully. In the past, this same question was asked by Sage Narada (a divine sage and devotee of Lord Vishnu who travels across realms) to Lord Brahma (the four-faced creator god in the Hindu Trinity). I shall now recount the same sacred story."

Narada said:

"O Four-faced one (Brahmaji), salutations! For the sake of properly worshipping Lord Vishnu (the Preserver in the Hindu Trinity), I wish to hear from your own mouth the details of the Ekadashi that falls in the bright half of the month of Bhadrapada."

Lord Brahma said:

"O Sage! You have asked a very noble question. Indeed, you are a true Vaishnava (devotee of Lord Vishnu), so it is natural for you to inquire about such matters. The Ekadashi that occurs in the Shukla Paksha of Bhadrapada is known as Padhā Ekadashi. On this holy day, Lord Hrishikesha (a name of Lord Vishnu meaning 'Lord of the senses') is worshipped with devotion. Observing this fast (vrata) brings great spiritual merit and is especially purifying."

"Now, let me tell you a wonderful story related to this sacred day."

In ancient times, in the Solar Dynasty (a royal lineage believed to descend from the Sun God), there lived a great king named Mandhāta. He was known for his truthfulness, piety, and strict adherence to dharma (righteous conduct). His kingdom was wealthy, disease-free, and the people were happy and spiritually inclined. There were no mental or physical afflictions, and the earth was as bountiful as Kamadhenu, the celestial wish-fulfilling cow.

However, due to the karmic effect of past deeds, his kingdom suddenly faced a severe drought — for three consecutive years, no rain fell. The crops failed, hunger spread, and the people were distressed. Unable to find relief, the citizens and sages of the land approached the king and said:

"O King! According to the ancient scriptures (Purāṇas), water is called 'Nara', and the Lord who dwells in water is called Nārāyaṇa (a name of Vishnu meaning 'He who rests on the waters'). He is the one who causes rain. Without rain, there is no food; and without food, even religious practices cannot be sustained. Please do something to restore balance and save your people."

The king humbly replied:

"You are right. Food is indeed life. Though I have ruled without injustice and have performed all duties according to dharma, I still see this calamity. Nevertheless, I will do whatever I can for the welfare of the kingdom."

King Mandhāta left his palace and, accompanied by a few trusted ministers, journeyed into the forest in search of a solution. There he visited many sages and hermitages until he finally encountered the great sage Angirā (one of the ancient seers mentioned in the Vedas).

Seeing the sage, the king got down from his chariot and bowed respectfully. After proper greetings, he explained his kingdom's situation.

Sage Angirā said:

"O King, you are indeed righteous, but this age is Satya Yuga (the first and purest of the four cosmic ages, where truth and virtue prevail). In this age, only brahmanas (priests and sages) are allowed to practice penance. However, in your kingdom, there is a shūdra (a person from the servant class) who is performing intense austerities. Though his intentions may not be wrong, such acts are not appropriate for his caste in this age. As a result, the natural order has been disrupted, and the rains have ceased."

The king replied:

"O Sage, though he may be outside the prescribed caste norms, he is not guilty of any harm. I cannot punish him. Please instruct me in a righteous way to remove the drought without causing harm to anyone."

Pleased by the king's compassion and integrity, Sage Angirā said:

"Then observe the vow of Padhā Ekadashi, which falls in the bright fortnight of Bhadrapada. If you and your subjects faithfully observe this fast and perform the proper rituals, the rains will return and prosperity will be restored."

King Mandhāta returned to his kingdom and, with all citizens — from all four varnas (castes) — observed the Padhā Ekadashi fast with devotion. As a result, clouds formed, rain poured down, and the earth became green and fertile once again. All were filled with joy and gratitude.

Lord Krishna concludes:

"O Yudhishthira, because of this history, the fast of Padhā Ekadashi is considered highly auspicious. On this day, one should offer a water-filled pot covered with a cloth to a brāhmaṇa (priest), along with curd, rice, an umbrella, and sandals. While making the offering, recite the following mantra:

"Namo namaste Govinda, Budhāvana-sanjñaka।
Aghaugha-saṅkṣayaṁ kṛtvā, sarva-saumya-prado bhava॥
Bhuṅkṣva muktiṁ ca me dehi, lokānāṁ sukhadāyaka॥"

Meaning:
"O Govinda (another name for Lord Vishnu), who is known as Budhāvana! I bow again and again to You. Please destroy all my sins, grant me all forms of well-being, and bless me with

both enjoyment and liberation. You are the giver of happiness to all living beings."

Meditation

"Close your eyes.
Feel yourself lying peacefully in the cosmic ocean.
As Lord Vishnu gently turns, feel your heart turning – from worldly attachments to divine longing.
Let go. Turn inward. Rest in the arms of the Infinite."

Mantra

Sanskrit: ॐ वामनाय नमः

Transliteration: "Om Vamanaya Namah"

Meaning: "Salutations to the Vamana form of Lord Vishnu, who holds the universe in three steps."

Chapter 25 — Indira Ekādaśī: Honoring the Ancestors 🌿

🪔 The Sacred Day of Ancestral Liberation — Indira Ekadashi

- **English Name:** Indira Ekadashi
- **Hindi Name:** इन्दिरा एकादशी
- **Pronunciation:** *In-dee-raa Ekaadashi*
- **Alternative Names:** Sometimes simply referred to as "Pitru Moksha Ekadashi" (पितृ मोक्ष एकादशी) in local traditions.

📅 Tithi and Timing

- **Hindu Calendar Tithi:** Āśvina Krishna Paksha Ekadashi (आश्विन कृष्ण पक्ष एकादशी)
- **Approximate Gregorian Calendar Timing:** September–October

🌙 Astronomical Note:

This Ekadashi falls in the waning phase of the moon during Pitru Paksha – the fortnight dedicated to honoring ancestors. Observances during this time are believed to deeply influence the ancestral realms.

✿ The Story of Indira Ekādaśī

Yudhishthira asked:
"O Madhusudana (another name of Lord Krishna, meaning 'slayer of the demon Madhu')! Kindly tell me, which Ekadashi falls in the Krishna Paksha (waning phase of the moon) of the month of Ashwin (a month in the Hindu calendar roughly corresponding to September-October)?"

Lord Shri Krishna replied:
"O King! In the Krishna Paksha of Ashwin month (according to the Gujarati and Maharashtrian calendars, it corresponds to *Bhadrapada*, a month in some regional Hindu calendars), the Ekadashi is called *Indira Ekadashi*. By observing the *vrat* (religious fast or vow) of this Ekadashi, even the gravest of sins (*maha-paap*) are destroyed. It grants liberation (*sadgati* – a good spiritual destination) even to ancestors (*pitrus*) who have fallen into lower births (*neech yoni* – lower or unfortunate forms of rebirth, considered due to bad karma).

O King! In ancient times, during the *Satya Yuga* (the first and purest of the four Hindu ages), there was a prince named *Indrasena*, who ruled the city of *Mahishmati* (a legendary city mentioned in many Hindu scriptures, often associated with righteousness and learning). He ruled his kingdom righteously and performed religious duties with great devotion. His fame had spread in all directions.

King Indrasena was deeply devoted to *Lord Vishnu* (the preserver among the Hindu Trinity). He spent his time chanting the liberating names of *Govinda* (a name of Krishna/Vishnu meaning protector of cows and the earth) and was immersed in spiritual contemplation (*adhyatma chintan* – deep thought on the nature of the Self and God). One day, while the king was sitting comfortably in his royal court, the divine sage *Narada* (a celestial sage known for his role as a messenger and devotee of Lord Vishnu) descended from the sky and arrived there. Upon seeing him, the king stood up with folded hands (*anjali mudra* – a gesture of respect), performed proper worship (*vidhi-purvak pooja*), and offered him a seat. Then he said:

"O revered sage (*Munivar*)! By your grace, all is well with me. Today, with your *darshan* (holy sight), all the merits of my sacrifices (*yajnas*) have become fruitful. O *Devarshi* (celestial sage)! Kindly bless me by revealing the purpose of your visit."

Narada said:
"O King! Listen. What I am about to tell you will surprise you. I had gone from *Brahmaloka* (the abode of Lord Brahma, the creator) to *Yamaloka* (the abode of Yama, the god of death). There, I was respectfully worshipped by *Yamaraja* (the divine judge of the dead) while seated on a grand throne. During that time, I saw your father in Yama's court. Due to the flaw of breaking a vow (*vrat-bhang dosh*), he had arrived there.

O King! He gave me a message for you. Listen carefully:
Son! Please deliver me to heaven (Swarga) by donating the merit (punya) of observing the Indira Ekadashi fast.
I have come to you with this message. O King! To deliver your father to the heavenly abode, observe the fast of *Indira Ekadashi*."

The king asked:
"O Lord! Kindly tell me how to perform the *Indira Ekadashi* fast — on which date (*tithi*),

during which lunar fortnight (*paksha*), and by what method (*vidhi*)?"

Narada replied:
"O King! Listen, I shall describe to you the auspicious method of this fast. In the Krishna Paksha of the month of Ashwin, on the *Dashami* (10th day), wake up early in the morning and bathe with a pure mind (*shuddha chitta*). Then, bathe again at midday, observe *ekabhukti* (take only one meal), and sleep on the floor (*bhoomi par shayan* – a form of austerity) at night.

At the end of the night, when dawn breaks, on the day of *Ekadashi*, clean your mouth with *datun* (herbal tooth-cleaning stick usually of Neem Tree) and wash your face. Then, with devotion (*bhakti bhava*), make a vow (*sankalp*) of fasting by reciting the following mantra:

"Agha sthitva niraaharaha sarva bhoga vivarjitaha |
Prabho aayae Pundarikaksha sharanam me bhava Achyuta ||"

Translation:
"O lotus-eyed Lord (*Pundarikaksha*) Narayana! Today, abstaining from all enjoyments and remaining without food (*nirahar*), I will eat

only tomorrow. O *Achyuta* (the infallible one)! I surrender myself to You."

Then, during midday, for the satisfaction of ancestors (*pitra-trupti*), perform *Shraddha* (ancestral rites) properly in front of a *Shalagrama Shila* (a sacred black stone considered a manifestation of Lord Vishnu). Honor Brahmins (*learned priests*) with gifts (*dakshina*) and serve them food. Offer the rice balls (*pindas*) prepared for ancestors to a cow after letting it smell them (*gau-daan is highly meritorious*).

Then worship *Lord Hrishikesha* (another name of Vishnu meaning 'Lord of the senses') with incense, fragrance, etc., and stay awake near Him throughout the night (*jagaran* – a night vigil dedicated to the deity). On the following day, *Dwadashi* (12th day), again worship *Lord Shri Hari* (Vishnu) with devotion. After this, feed Brahmins and then, along with brothers, relatives, grandchildren, and sons, take your meal in silence (*mauna bhojan* – symbolic of spiritual absorption).

O King! Perform this fast without negligence (*aalasya-rahit*). By doing so, your father will attain *Vaikuntha Dham* (the supreme eternal abode of Lord Vishnu, free from all suffering)."

Lord Shri Krishna concluded:
"O King! After hearing this, sage *Narada* disappeared. King *Indrasena*, along with his queens, sons, and servants, faithfully observed this supreme fast as described.

O *Kuntinandana* (son of Kunti, i.e., Yudhishthira)! When the fast was completed, flowers began to shower from the sky (*divine sign of approval*). Indrasena's father ascended to *Shri Vishnu Dham* riding on *Garuda* (the celestial eagle and vehicle of Vishnu), and King Indrasena himself ruled his kingdom happily, free from all troubles. Eventually, he installed his son on the throne and departed for heaven.

In this way, I have narrated to you the greatness (*mahatmya*) of the *Indira Ekadashi* fast. By reading or listening to this story, a person becomes free from all sins (*sarva paap mukti*).

Meditation

"Sit quietly.
Visualize a river of golden light flowing from your heart to the ancestral worlds.
Offer love, prayers, and light to every soul connected to you.

Feel the burdens lifting, the river carrying all pain away, merging into the Infinite."

🌿 Mantra

Sanskrit:

ॐ पितृभ्यः स्वधा नमः

Transliteration:

"Om Pitrubhyah Swadhā Namah"

Meaning:

Obeisance and offerings to the revered ancestors.

Chapter 26 — Pāpaṅkuśa Ekādaśī: The Destroyer of Sins 🌿

🔥 The Sacred Day of Sin Dissolution — Papankusha Ekadashi

- **English Name:** Papankusha Ekadashi
- **Hindi Name:** पापांकुश एकादशी
- **Pronunciation:** *Paap-ankusha Ekaadashi*
- **Alternative Names:** Sometimes known as "Ashwina Shukla Ekadashi" (आश्विन शुक्ल एकादशी)

📅 Tithi and Timing

- **Hindu Calendar Tithi:** Āshvina Shukla Paksha Ekadashi (आश्विन शुक्ल पक्ष एकादशी)
- **Approximate Gregorian Calendar Timing:** September–October

🌙 Astronomical Note:

This Ekadashi arises during the waxing phase of the moon, coinciding with the Navaratri (nine days of fast devoted to nine forms of

Supreme Goddess Durga) – a time when spiritual efforts are greatly magnified.

✿ The Story of Pāpaṅkuśa Ekādaśī

Yudhishthira asked: O Madhusudana! Now, please tell me which Ekadashi occurs in the Shukla Paksha of Ashwin and what is its significance?

Lord Krishna replied: O King! The Ekadashi that occurs in the Shukla Paksha (the waxing phase of the moon) of Ashwin (the seventh month of the Hindu lunar calendar, typically falling around September-October) is known as 'Papankusha' Ekadashi (the Ekadashi that drives away sins). It is the one that eradicates all sins, grants liberation and salvation, makes the body disease-free, and provides beauty, wealth, and prosperity. Even if a person performs other activities but worships this Ekadashi alone, he will never undergo the tortures of Yama (the god of death in Hinduism).

O King! A person who fasts and stays awake during the night on this Ekadashi day, will, without effort, become divine in form, with four arms, adorned with a flag of Garuda (a divine bird associated with Lord Vishnu), shining with a necklace, and dressed in yellow garments, and will reach the abode of Lord Vishnu (a deity in Hinduism, considered the protector and preserver of the universe). O King! Such a person liberates ten generations on the maternal side, ten generations on the paternal side, and even ten generations on the side of his wife. On that day, one should worship Me, Vaasudeva (a name for Lord Krishna), to fulfill all desires. The result that a person gains by performing severe penance for ages is obtained simply by worshipping Lord Garuda-Dhwaj (Vishnu), the flag-bearer.

One who donates gold, sesame (a sacred seed used in Hindu rituals), land, cows, food, water, shoes, and umbrellas (items considered charitable in Hinduism) will never see Yama. O King! A person should also make his day successful by performing bathing, chanting (the repetition of sacred mantras), meditation, sacrifices, and donations after performing these sacred activities.

Those who perform sacrifices (ritual offerings to deities), bathing (ritual purification), chanting, meditation, and other pious deeds do not have to face the terrible tortures of Yama. Those who are seen as long-lived, wealthy, noble, and disease-free in the world are actually those who have accumulated past merits (good deeds done in previous lives). Pious individuals are seen in this way. What is the benefit of saying more about this subject? People who indulge in sin fall into greater misfortune and go to hell (a realm of suffering in Hindu belief).

O King! I have explained the significance of 'Papankusha Ekadashi' as you asked. Now, is there anything else you wish to hear?

🛕 Meditation

"Visualize a brilliant lotus blossoming in your heart,
Holding a golden ankush (goad) made of light.
With every breath, use it to gently push away all inner shadows and negativity,
Guiding your soul toward the effulgent Vishnu who awaits beyond."

🏵 Mantra

Sanskrit: ॐ पद्मनाभाय नमः

Transliteration: "Om Padmanabhaya Namah"

Meaning: "Salutations to the Lotus-Naveled Lord."

Chapter 27 – Rāma Ekādaśī: The Sweet Name of Rāma

✿ The Sacred Day of Divine Grace — Rama Ekadashi

- **English Name:** Rama Ekadashi
- **Hindi Name:** रमा एकादशी
- **Pronunciation:** *Rāma Ekaadashī*

Tithi and Timing

- **Hindu Calendar Tithi:** Kārtika Krishna Paksha Ekadashi (कार्तिक कृष्ण पक्ष एकादशी)
- **Approximate Gregorian Calendar Timing:** October–November

Astronomical Note:

Rama Ekadashi occurs during the waning phase of the moon in Kartika – the holiest month in the Hindu calendar, charged with sacred vibrations.

✿ The Story of Rāma Ekādaśī

Yudhishthir asked:
"Janardan (a name of Lord Vishnu, meaning 'one who helps people')! You have affection for me, therefore please tell me—which Ekadashi falls in the Krishna Paksha (waning phase of the moon) of Kartik month (a holy Hindu lunar month, usually around October–November)?"

Bhagwan Shri Krishna said:
"O King! In the Krishna Paksha of Kartik (according to Gujarat and Maharashtra, this corresponds to the month of Ashvin), the renowned and supremely auspicious Ekadashi named *Rama* occurs. It is of the highest merit and capable of destroying even the gravest of sins."

"In ancient times, there was a famous king named *Muchukund*, who was a devotee of Bhagwan (Lord) Shri Vishnu (the preserver deity in the Hindu trinity) and a speaker of truth. He ruled his kingdom without obstacle. In his lineage, the river gave rise to a daughter named *Chandrabhaga* (a princess said to be born of the river). The king married her to a prince named *Shobhan*, son of Chandrasena.

One time, Shobhan came to his father-in-law's house on the day of Dashami (10th lunar day, one day before Ekadashi). On that same day, it was proclaimed throughout the entire city: No one shall consume food on Ekadashi. Upon hearing this, Shobhan said to his beloved wife Chandrabhaga: Dear, now teach me—what should I do at this time?"

Chandrabhaga said:
"Lord! In my father's household, not even domestic animals eat on Ekadashi. O protector of my life! If you eat, you will face great criticism. So reflect in your heart and make your resolve firm."

Shobhan said:
"Dear, your words are true. I too shall fast. Whatever is destined by Daiva (divine will or fate) shall come to pass."

Shri Krishna said:
"In this way, making a firm resolution, Shobhan followed the vow of the fast. But before sunrise, he passed away. King Muchukund performed his Raj-uchit Dah Sanskar (royal funeral rites). Chandrabhaga, after completing her husband's Paralaukik Karma (rituals for the soul's post-death journey), continued to live at her father's home."

"O King! Due to the power of that Vrata (vow or sacred observance), Shobhan attained a Divya Nagar (heavenly city) situated on the peak of Mount Mandarachal (a mythical sacred mountain mentioned in Hindu texts). There, he shone with splendor like another Kubera (the Hindu god of wealth).

Once, a renowned Brahmin (a member of the priestly class in Hindu society) from King Muchukund's city named Somsharma, while on Tirtha-Yatra (pilgrimage to sacred places), came to Mount Mandarachal, where he saw Shobhan. Recognizing his king's son-in-law, he approached him. Shobhan too, upon seeing the respected Somsharma, rose from his seat and offered him respect. Then he inquired about his father-in-law King Muchukund, his dear wife Chandrabhaga, and the well-being of the entire city."

Somsharma said:
"O King! Everyone is well there. Astonishing! I have never seen a city as beautiful and unique as this. Please tell me—how did you attain such a city?"

Shobhan said:
"O Rishi (sage)! By observing the Rama Ekadashi, which falls in the Krishna Paksha of Kartik, I attained this divine city. O Brahmin!

Since I observed this excellent fast without full awareness, I believe this city is not permanent. Kindly go and tell this entire account to Chandrabhaga, the beautiful daughter of King Muchukund."

After hearing this, the Brahmin Somsharma returned to Muchukund's city and narrated the entire account to Chandrabhaga.

Somsharma said:
"Dear! I saw your husband with my own eyes. I also saw his city, which is like Indrapuri (city of Indra, king of the gods), but it is not permanent. You must make it stable."

Chandrabhaga said:
"O Brahmin! I have a strong desire to see my husband. Please take me there. By the merit of my fasting vows, I will make that city permanent."

Shri Krishna said:
"O King! Hearing this, Somsharma took her with him to the hermitage of sage Vamadeva (a revered ancient sage) near Mount Mandarachal. There, due to the sage's Mantra-Shakti (spiritual power derived from sacred chants) and the effect of Ekadashi observance, Chandrabhaga's body became Divya (divine), and she attained divine status. Then she went

to her husband. Seeing his beloved wife arrive, Shobhan was overjoyed. He called her and seated her on the throne beside him."

"Then Chandrabhaga said these truthful words to her dear husband:
'O Lord! Please listen to my beneficial words. From the time I turned eight, I have been observing Ekadashi fasts continuously. By the Punya (spiritual merit) accumulated from those fasts, this city shall remain eternal until the end of the Kalpa (about 4.32 billion years), and it shall always be filled with all kinds of desired prosperity.'"

O King!
In this way, due to the effect of the Rama Ekadashi fast, Chandrabhaga, adorned with Divya Bhoga (heavenly pleasures), Divya Roop (divine form), and Divya Aabhushan (celestial ornaments), lives with her husband on the peak of Mount Mandarachal. O King! I have narrated to you the story of the Ekadashi named Rama. It is like the Chintamani (a mythical wish-fulfilling gem) and Kamadhenu (a divine cow that grants all desires), and fulfills all wishes.

🛕 Meditation

"Visualize a bridge of radiant gold emerging from your heart, stretching toward the Infinite. Each breath carries the sacred name 'Rāma', placing one step after another across this bridge.
Feel yourself walking with effortless joy, moving closer to the Divine Light."

🏵 Mantra

Sanskrit: श्री रामाय नमः

Transliteration: "Sri Ramaya Namah"

Meaning: "Salutations to Sri Rama, the embodiment of dharma and compassion."

Chapter 28 — Devutthāna Ekādaśī: Divine Awakening

- **English Name:** Devutthana Ekadashi
- **Hindi Name:** देवुत्थान एकादशी
- **Pronunciation:** *Devutthāna Ekaadashī*
- **Alternative Names:** Prabodhini Ekadashi (प्रबोधिनी एकादशी), Hari Prabodhini Ekadashi.

Tithi and Timing

- **Hindu Calendar Tithi:** Kārtika Shukla Paksha Ekadashi (कार्तिक शुक्ल पक्ष एकादशी)
- **Approximate Gregorian Calendar Timing:** October–November

Astronomical Note:

Devutthana Ekadashi falls as the lunar energies swell during the waxing phase of Kartika, enhancing both mental alertness and spiritual receptivity.

The Story of Devutthāna Ekādaśī

Bhagwan Shri Krishna said:
"O Arjuna! I will narrate to you the conversation that took place between Narada and Brahma regarding the 'Prabodhini Ekadashi' of the Shukla Paksha (the bright fortnight of the moon) in the month of Kartik (a sacred Hindu month, usually October–November), which bestows liberation."

Once, Naradji asked Brahmaji:
"O Father! Please kindly tell me in detail about the fruits of observing the Prabodhini Ekadashi Vrat (a religious vow involving fasting and worship on the 11th lunar day)."

Brahmaji said:
"O Son! That which is extremely difficult to attain even in the higher worlds can be obtained through the Vrat of Prabodhini Ekadashi in the Kartik month's Shukla Paksha. Due to the power of this Vrat (sacred fast), numerous sins from past births are destroyed instantly.
O Son! The little merit (Punya) (spiritual credit or good karma) a person performs sincerely on this day becomes immovable like a mountain. Their ancestors attain Vishnuloka (the divine realm of Lord Vishnu). Even great sins like Brahmahatya (killing a Brahmin,

considered one of the gravest sins) are destroyed by Jagaran (staying awake the entire night in devotion) on the night of Prabodhini Ekadashi.
O Narada! For the pleasure of Bhagwan (God, especially Lord Vishnu in this context), one must certainly observe this Ekadashi Vrat in the month of Kartik. One who observes this Vrat becomes wealthy, a Yogi (spiritually disciplined person), a Tapasvi (one who practices austerities), and victorious over the senses, because Ekadashi is extremely dear to Lord Vishnu (the preserver deity in Hinduism).

On this day, those who perform charity, Tap (penance), Homa (fire ritual), and Yajna (sacrifice, especially chanting God's names) attain Akshaya Punya (imperishable spiritual merit). Chanting the Lord's names is itself the greatest Yajna – as stated in the Bhagavad Gita, "Yajnanam japa-yajno'smi" (Of all sacrifices, I am the sacrifice of chanting).

Therefore, O Narada! You must also properly worship Lord Vishnu. On the day of this Ekadashi, one should rise during Brahma Muhurta (pre-dawn spiritual hour), take a vow (Sankalp) (formal intention for the fast), and perform worship. At night, one should stay near the deity and spend time singing, dancing, storytelling, and performing Kirtan (devotional music).

On Prabodhini Ekadashi, one should offer flowers, incense (agar), and lamps (dhoop) to the Lord, and present Naivedya (devotional food offering). The spiritual benefit of this is millions of times greater than going on pilgrimages or giving charity.

Those who worship Lord Vishnu with rose (*Rosa spp.*), bakul (*Mimusops elengi*), ashoka (*Saraca asoca*), white and red kaner (*Nerium oleander*), durva grass (*Cynodon dactylon*), shami leaves (*Prosopis cineraria* or *Ficus religiosa*, depending on region), and champaka flowers (*Magnolia champaca*) are freed from the cycle of birth and death (reincarnation or samsara).

Those who had given up something during the Chaturmasya Vrat (a four-month period of spiritual discipline and austerity) should resume it on this day. Anyone who sincerely observes Prabodhini Ekadashi Vrat gains eternal happiness and ultimately reaches Swarga (heaven)."

Spiritual Significance

1. Waking of Lord Vishnu:
   On this day, it is believed that Lord Vishnu awakens from his cosmic sleep (Yoga Nidra), which began on Devshayani Ekadashi (in Ashadha month). This awakening is called 'Prabodhini' or 'Uthapana'.

2. Resumption of Auspicious Ceremonies:
   During Chaturmas (the four months Vishnu is asleep), weddings, housewarmings, thread ceremonies, and other major rituals are avoided. After Devuthan Ekadashi, these can resume.

3. Vishnu & Tulsi Marriage (Tulsi Vivah):
   A symbolic wedding of the sacred Tulsi plant (Ocimum tenuiflorum) to Lord Vishnu (in the form of Shaligram stone) is performed, representing the union of the divine feminine and masculine energies.

4. Path to Liberation (Moksha):
   Observing a fast (Ekadashi Vrat), keeping vigil at night, and worshipping Lord Vishnu on this day is believed to cleanse sins and help attain moksha (liberation from the cycle of rebirth).

Step-by-Step Tulsi Vivah Ritual

1. Preparation

Time to start: Ideally in the morning or evening.
Location: A clean, quiet space in your home, such as a small altar, windowsill, or garden.

Items needed (or substitutes):

- A healthy Tulsi plant in a pot (represents the bride)
- A small idol of Vishnu or a Shaligram stone (represents the groom)
- Red cloth or scarf (to dress Tulsi as a bride)
- Yellow cloth (to dress the Vishnu idol)
- Flowers or garlands
- A cotton thread or ribbon (for symbolic union)
- A small metal pot of water (represents holy water)
- Sweets or fruits (as offerings)
- Diya (oil lamp) or candle
- Incense stick (optional)
- A small bell (optional)

2. Clean and Decorate the Space

- Clean the area where the ritual will take place.
- Place the Tulsi plant and Vishnu idol/Shaligram side by side, as if the bride and groom are seated.
- Decorate Tulsi with the red cloth and garlands.
- Wrap the Vishnu idol/Shaligram with the yellow cloth and flowers.

3. Invocation and Lighting

- Light a diya (oil lamp) or candle.
- Optionally, ring a small bell to invite divine presence.
- Close your eyes, take a deep breath, and mentally offer your intentions (peace, devotion, love, spiritual blessings).

4. The Symbolic Wedding

1. Apply a pinch of turmeric and vermilion to the Tulsi plant (optional).
2. Tie a thread or ribbon from the Tulsi stalk to the Vishnu idol. This signifies their union.

3. Exchange garlands (or place one flower on each).
4. Say:

"I perform the divine wedding of Goddess Tulsi and Lord Vishnu with devotion. May this union bless all beings with love, harmony, and spiritual awakening."

5. Offerings and Prayer

- Offer sweets or fruits to both Tulsi and Vishnu.
- Offer water using the small pot (just sprinkle a little near each).
- Light the incense (optional).
- Recite any of these short prayers (or your own):

"*Om Namo Bhagavate Vasudevaya*" (Salutations to Lord Vishnu)
"*Tulasi Devi Namastubhyam*" (Salutations to Goddess Tulsi)

- Sit silently for a moment with hands folded.

6. Aarti and Completion

- Wave the diya (lamp or candle) in circular motion (clockwise) in front of the deities.

- Ring the bell (if available).
- Share the offerings (prasad) with family and friends.
- Optionally, donate food, clothes, or money to someone in need as a gesture of goodwill.

Meditation

"Visualize the first golden rays of dawn striking the heart.
As the golden light rises, feel Lord Vishnu awakening within your soul.
With each breath, the lotus of your being blooms toward the cosmic sky."

Mantra

Sanskrit: उठो देव जगत्पते विष्णो लोकानां पते प्रभो

Transliteration: "Utho Deva Jagatpate Vishno Lokanam Patey Prabho"

Meaning: "Awaken, O Lord of the Universe, O Vishnu, O Master of all worlds!"

Chapter 29 — Parama Ekadashi: The Supreme Grace of Adhik Maas 🌿

✨ The Sacred Day of Supreme Purity — Parama Ekadashi

- **English Name:** Parama Ekadashi
- **Hindi Name:** परमा एकादशी
- **Pronunciation:** Puh-ruh-muh Eh-kaa-dush-ee

📅 Tithi and Timing

• **Hindu Calendar Tithi:** Krishna Paksha Ekadashi of **Adhik Maas** (Extra Month)
• **Approximate Gregorian Calendar:** Varies – Adhik Maas occurs approximately every **2 years, 8 months, and 16 days**, and may fall in **July–September** based on astronomical calculations.

🌿 Astronomical Note:

Adhik Maas ("Extra Month"), is inserted to synchronize the lunar calendar with the solar year. It is a sacred time of pause, reflection, and intense sadhana, when material ventures are minimized, and inner spiritual work is emphasized.

The Story of Parama Ekadashi

Arjuna said:
"O Janardana (another name for Lord Krishna, meaning 'one who is the sustainer of people')! Please tell me the name of the Ekadashi that falls during the Krishna Paksha (the dark/waxing phase of the moon) of the Adhik Maas (also called Mal Maas or Purushottam Maas), and describe the method of observing its vrat (religious fast). Which deity (god) is worshipped on this Ekadashi, and what are the results of observing this vrat?"

Shri Krishna replied:
"O Partha (another name for Arjuna)! The name of this Ekadashi is 'Parama'. By observing this vrat, all paap (sins) are destroyed, and one attains sukh (happiness) in this life and moksha (liberation from the cycle of birth and death) in the afterlife. On this day, one should worship Lord Vishnu (the preserver god in the Hindu trinity) with dhoop (incense), deep (lamps), naivedya (food offerings), pushpa (flowers), and other devotional items.

Now I will narrate a beautiful story associated with this Ekadashi that took place in Kampilya

Nagari (an ancient Indian city), in the presence of sages. Listen carefully:

In the city of Kampilya, lived a very righteous Brahmin (member of the priestly class), named Sumedha. His wife was extremely virtuous and devoted to her husband. However, due to some past-life karma (actions that influence future experiences), the couple lived in extreme daridra (poverty). The Brahmin's wife served him with great devotion and often gave food to guests while going hungry herself.

One day, Sumedha said to his wife:
"O noble one! A householder's life cannot continue without wealth. Therefore, I will go to a distant place and engage in some udyog (business or enterprise)."

She replied:
"O beloved! A wife should obey whatever her husband says—be it good or bad. A person reaps the fruits of their actions of previous lives. What fate or divine will has written in one's destiny cannot be changed. O dear husband! There is no need for you to go elsewhere. Whatever is destined will come to us right here."

Accepting her advice, Sumedha did not leave for a foreign land.

At that time, the sage Kaudinya Muni (a revered Hindu sage or seer) arrived in their area. Seeing him, Sumedha and his wife offered respectful pranam (greetings with folded hands) and said,
"Today, we are blessed! Our life has become successful upon seeing you."
They offered the sage a seat and food.

After the meal, the virtuous wife said:
"O great sage! You have come to us by our good fortune. I am now confident that our poverty will soon end. Please show us a way to overcome this poverty."

Kaudinya Muni said:
"By observing the Parama Ekadashi vrat during the Krishna Paksha of Adhik Maas, all sins, sufferings, and poverty are removed. The person who performs this vrat becomes wealthy. This vrat should be performed with kirtan (devotional singing), bhajan (devotional music), and jagaran (staying awake through the night in worship). Mahadeva (another name for Lord Shiva) made Kubera (the god of wealth) the Dhanadhyaksha (treasurer of the gods) by the power of this very vrat."

Then Kaudinya Muni explained the procedure for performing the Parama Ekadashi vrat.
He said:

"O Brahmani (wife of a Brahmin)! On this day, after performing the nitya karma (daily spiritual duties such as bathing and prayer), begin the Pancha Ratri Vrat (a five-night religious observance) with proper rituals. Those who observe this vrat for five days with nirjala vrat (fasting without food or water) go to Swargalok (heaven) along with their mata-pita (mother and father) and spouse. O Brahmani! Perform this vrat with your husband. You will surely attain success and, ultimately, Swarga (heaven)."

Following the instructions of Kaudinya Muni, the couple observed the Parama Ekadashi vrat for five days.
After completing the vrat, the Brahmin's wife saw a prince approaching.
Inspired by the punya (merit) of the Brahmin, the prince granted them a village for livelihood and a beautiful house fully equipped with everything they needed.

Through the merit of this vrat, the couple enjoyed great happiness in this world and ultimately attained Swargalok (the celestial realms).

O Partha!
Whoever observes the Parama Ekadashi vrat gains the combined spiritual merit or result of

all pilgrimage places and yagyas (Vedic rituals or fire sacrifices).
Just as among four-legged animals, the cow is supreme, and among the gods, Indra (king of the heavens) is supreme, similarly among all months, Adhik Maas is the most sacred.
The Panch Ratri vrat performed during this month brings immense merit. Also, the Parinee Ekadashi observed in this month is of the highest value.
By observing it, all sins are destroyed, and one attains punya lokas (virtuous heavenly realms).

Meditation

"Close your eyes and visualize Lord Vishnu reclining on the cosmic ocean, resting upon Ananta Shesha, infinite stars sparkling around Him. Inhale deeply: feel the entire universe dissolve into the Lord's breath. Exhale: offer your small self into His infinite light."

Mantra

Sanskrit:

ॐ अपवित्रः पवित्रो वा सर्वावस्थां गतोऽपि वा।

यः स्मरेत् पुण्डरीकाक्षं स बाह्याभ्यन्तरः शुचिः॥

Transliteration:

"Om Apavitrah Pavitro Va Sarvavastham
Gato'pi Va,
Yah Smaret Pundarikaksham Sa
Bahyabhyantarah Shuchih."

Meaning: Whether pure or impure, remembering the Lotus-Eyed Vishnu purifies internally and externally.

Chapter 30 – Padmini Ekadashi: The Blossoming of Eternal Devotion 🌿

✿ The Day of the Sacred Lotus – Padmini Ekadashi

- **English Name:** Padmini Ekadashi
- **Hindi Name:** पद्मिनी एकादशी
- **Pronunciation (Phonetic):** Puhd-mee-nee Eh-kaa-dush-ee

📅 Tithi and Timing

• **Hindu Calendar Tithi:** Shukla Paksha Ekadashi of Adhik Maas (the extra month)
• **Approximate Gregorian Calendar:** Falls during the rare Adhik Maas, generally between July and September, based on astronomical alignments.

🌿 Astronomical Note:

Adhik Maas is inserted to correct the mismatch between the lunar and solar calendars, aligning cosmic energies with earthly time.

The Story of Padmini Ekadashi

Arjuna said:
"O Lord! Now please tell me about the *Ekadashi* of the Shukla Paksha (bright fortnight of the moon) during the Adhik Maas. What is its name, what is the procedure of observing it? Which deity is worshiped, and what result does it bring?"

Shri Krishna said:
"O Partha (Arjuna)! The Ekadashi in Adhik Maas bestows many spiritual merits. Its name is Padmini Ekadashi. Observing its fast leads a person to Vaikuntha (the eternal abode of Lord Vishnu in Hindu belief). It destroys numerous sins and grants liberation (Moksha) and devotion (Bhakti). Now, listen carefully to its benefits and process:

The fast should begin on Dashami (10th day of the lunar fortnight). On Ekadashi, after morning duties, one should go to a punya kshetra (sacred pilgrimage site) for a ritual bath. The bath is to be taken using cow dung (considered purifying), sacred mud, sesame seeds, Kusha grass (a type of holy grass used in rituals) and Amla powder (Indian gooseberry, a sacred plant in Ayurveda).

Before bathing, apply sacred mud to the body while offering a prayer like this:
"O sacred Earth! I bow to you. May my body be purified by your touch. Born from medicinal herbs, cleanser of the Earth, please sanctify me.
O Lord of Lords! Holder of the conch (shankha), discus (chakra), and mace (gada), O Jagannatha (Lord of the Universe, another name for Vishnu), please grant me permission to bathe."

After that, chant the Varuna mantra (a hymn invoking Varuna, the god of water), and if a sacred river isn't nearby, bathe in any water body while remembering sacred rivers. After the bath, wear clean clothes, perform Sandhya (evening prayer), Tarpan (water offerings to ancestors), and then go to a temple to worship the Lord with incense (dhoop), lamp (deep), food offerings (naivedya), flowers, saffron, and more.

Then, sing and dance before the Lord. With fellow devotees, listen to Puranic stories (narratives from ancient Hindu scriptures). On this day, the fast should ideally be observed as Nirjala (without even water). If that's not possible, one may take water or light food.

At night, one must perform Jagran (staying awake in devotional singing and remembrance of God). During the four quarters of the night, worship Vishnu or Shiva with different offerings:

- 1st quarter: Offer coconut.
- 2nd quarter: Offer Bilva fruit (sacred to Lord Shiva).
- 3rd quarter: Offer custard apple (sitaphal).
- 4th quarter: Offer betel nut (supari) and orange.

Each of these offerings brings results equivalent to performing ancient Vedic sacrifices:

- Agni-homa (fire ritual)
- Vajapeya Yajna (a high-level royal sacrifice)
- Ashvamedha Yajna (symbolic horse sacrifice ritual by kings)
- Rajasuya Yajna (coronation and imperial sacrifice)

There is no greater penance, charity, or sacrifice than this Ekadashi fast. The one who observes it receives the merit of all pilgrimages (*tirthas*) and sacrifices (*yajnas*).

One should stay awake until sunrise, then bathe and offer meals to Brahmins (priests and scholars in Hindu tradition). A person who worships the Lord and fasts properly on this day lives a successful life, enjoys worldly happiness, and ultimately attains Vishnu's supreme abode (Vaikuntha).

"O Partha! I have now told you the complete observance method (*Vrat Vidhi*) of this Ekadashi."

The Story Behind the Vrat:

Now I shall tell you a tale of one who faithfully observed Padmini Ekadashi. Listen carefully. This story was narrated by Sage Pulastya to Narada Muni:

Once, King Kartavirya (a mighty and divine king) captured Ravana (the demon king of Lanka, antagonist in the Ramayana) and imprisoned him. When Sage Pulastya humbly requested, Ravana was released. Hearing this, Narada asked:
"O great sage! Ravana defeated the gods themselves – how did Kartavirya overpower him? Please explain."

Pulastya said:
"There once lived King Kritavirya, who had 100 wives but no worthy son. Despite conducting many Yajnas (sacrificial rituals for divine blessings), he remained childless. Saddened, he renounced the world and went to the forest for tapasya (intense meditation and austerities). His wife, Poomda (daughter of Harishchandra), also left her ornaments and followed him to Mount Gandhamadana (a mythological mountain).

There, they performed penance for 10,000 years. The king had become skeletal. Seeing this, Poomda asked the great chaste woman Anusuya why the gods had not blessed them with a child.

Anusuya replied:
"O dear! Every 36 months, an extra month (Adhik or Mal Maas) occurs. In this month, there are two special Ekadashis:

- Shukla Paksha Ekadashi is called Padmini,
- Krishna Paksha Ekadashi is called Parama.

If you fast and perform night vigil during these, the Lord will surely bless you."

Anusuya taught her the rituals. The queen followed her advice and observed Padmini Ekadashi properly, staying awake through the night. Lord Vishnu appeared, pleased, and asked for her wish.

She replied:
"Please grant a boon to my husband."

Lord Vishnu said:
"O Poomda! The Adhik Maas is extremely dear to me. And among all, Ekadashi in this month is my favorite. You've observed it correctly, so I am deeply pleased."

The Lord then turned to the king and said:
"Ask for any boon. Your wife has pleased me."

The king said:
"O Lord! Grant me a son who is peerless, revered by all, and invincible to gods, demons, and humans – except for You."

Vishnu blessed him, saying "Tathastu" (So be it), and vanished.

The couple returned to their kingdom, and later, Kartavirya was born – the one who defeated Ravana.
This was the fruit of Padmini Ekadashi's observance.

Pulastya concluded the tale and left.

Lord Krishna said:
“O Arjuna, son of Pandu! This is the sacred Vrat (vow/fast) of Padmini Ekadashi, which falls in the Shukla Paksha of Adhik/Mal/Purushottam Maas.
Whoever performs this Vrat with devotion will attain Vaikuntha, the eternal abode of Lord Vishnu.”

🏵 Meditation

"Sit in silence.
Visualize a golden lotus blooming at your heart center.
Upon this lotus, see Lord Vishnu, radiant, smiling, holding conch, discus, mace, and lotus.
With each inhalation, let the petals open;
With each exhalation, surrender all impurities into His hands.
Feel yourself merged into the vast ocean of bliss."

🌼 Mantra

Sanskrit:

यः करोति महापुण्यं पद्मिनी एकादशी व्रतम्।

स सर्वपापविनिर्मुक्तः विष्णुलोकं स गच्छति॥

Transliteration:

"Yaḥ karoti mahāpuṇyaṁ Padminī Ekādaśī vratam,
Sa sarvapāpavinirmuktaḥ Viṣṇulokaṁ sa gacchati."

Meaning:

He who observes the highly meritorious fast of Padmini Ekadashi,
Is freed from all sins and goes to the abode of Lord Vishnu.

Chapter 31 — Temples of Ekadashi Worship Across India 🌿

🌷 Introduction: The Sacred Geography of Ekadashi

Across the vast and sacred land of Bharatavarsha (India), countless temples resonate with the divine energy of Ekadashi. While Lord Vishnu is worshipped every day, Ekadashi holds a special place, and numerous temples celebrate this tithi (sacred day) with grandeur, devotion, and ancient rituals.

These holy shrines are not merely architectural marvels — they are living energy centers, pulsating with vibrations accumulated over millennia.

🏵 Major Temples Associated with Ekadashi Observances

Here is a list of temples highlighting the places and significance:

1. Jagannath Temple

Place: Puri, Odisha
Significance: Known for *Anavasara rituals* during Ekadashi; the deity is not available for darshan on specific Ekadashi days.

---

2. Pandharpur Vitthal Temple

Place: Pandharpur, Maharashtra
Significance: Celebrates Ashadhi Ekadashi with a massive Wari yatra, where millions of devotees walk for days to reach the temple.

---

3. Tirupati Balaji Temple

Place: Tirupati, Andhra Pradesh
Significance: Features special pujas, Abhisheka, and Vishnu Sahasranama chanting on Ekadashi.

---

4. Dwarkadhish Temple

Place: Dwarka, Gujarat
Significance: The Dwarkadhish deity is richly adorned, and special aartis and darshan take place on Ekadashi.

---

5. Srirangam Ranganathaswamy Temple

Place: Srirangam, Tamil Nadu
Significance: On Vaikunta Ekadashi, the sacred Vaikunta Dwara (gateway to heaven) is opened, symbolizing entry to salvation.

---

6. Udupi Krishna Matha

Place: Udupi, Karnataka
Significance: Celebrated with intense fasting, devotional singing (bhajans), and Tulasi Archana.

---

7. Padmanabhaswamy Temple

Place: Thiruvananthapuram, Kerala
Significance: Hosts grand Ekadashi festivals, especially Vaikunta Ekadashi, with elaborate rituals and temple processions.

🏵 Unique Rituals on Ekadashi at Temples

- Jagran (Night Vigil): Mass chanting and singing throughout the night.
- Special Abhishekas: Milk, curd, honey, ghee, sugar, and Tulasi used.

- Tulasi Archana: Thousand-leaf Tulasi offering to the deity.
- Vishnu Sahasranama Parayana: Recitation of the thousand names of Vishnu.

🏵 Suggested Pilgrimage Flow

If one wishes to plan an Ekadashi Pilgrimage, it is auspicious to visit:

- Tirupati → Pandharpur → Dwarka → Puri → Srirangam → Padmanabhaswamy
  (all linked to different forms of Vishnu worship).

Even mental pilgrimage (मनः यात्रा) — imagining the darshan at these temples — grants spiritual merit if actual travel is not possible.

🛕 Some More Sacred Temples Honoring Ekadashi

- **Badrinath Temple**, Uttarakhand — Vishnu as the Himalayan sage.
- **Govind Dev Ji Temple**, Jaipur — Celebrations in Pushtimarg tradition.

- **Ranchhodraiji Temple**, Dakor – Gujarati Vaishnava tradition.
- **Guruvayur Temple**, Kerala – Krishna worship on all Ekadashis.

Each of these places becomes a gateway to the Infinite, especially on this sacred day.

🏵 Final Reflection

"Wherever Vishnu is worshiped with devotion,
There is Ekadashi.
Wherever Ekadashi is observed,
There dwells eternal Vaikuntha."

Chapter 32 – Conclusion

A Journey Beyond Time

The path of Ekadashi is more than a calendar of fasts – it is a pilgrimage of the soul through time. Each observance invites us to step away from the noise of the world and into the quiet sanctuary of inner stillness. It teaches us that sacredness lies not only in rituals, but in the intention behind them.

From the birth of the Divine Mother on Utpanna Ekadashi to the awakening of Lord Vishnu on Devutthāna, we have traced a spiritual arc that mirrors the cycle of life itself – from creation to rest, from desire to detachment, from struggle to liberation.

Through fasting, prayer, and reflection, Ekadashi becomes a mirror – showing us our attachments, our resilience, and ultimately our longing to return to the divine center within. Whether you are a seeker of knowledge, a devotee of tradition, or simply curious about ancient wisdom, Ekadashi welcomes all who are willing to pause and listen.

In honoring Ekadashi, we do not merely follow time — we transcend it.

Let every Ekadashi be not an obligation, but a celebration of what is eternal.

With reverence,
let the fast become a feast of the soul.

ॐ नमो भगवते वासुदेवाय

Om Namo Bhagavate Vasudevaya
"I bow to Lord Vasudeva (Vishnu), the Supreme Being."

Thank You for Reading!

I'm deeply grateful that you took the time to read *Ekadashi – The Eleventh Day: Tuning Inner Waters to the Cosmic Ocean.*

If the book resonated with you, I would truly appreciate your honest review on Amazon. Your thoughts help other seekers discover this work—and help me continue sharing spiritual reflections.

Scan the QR Code below to leave a review

—or—

Visit this link:

https://www.amazon.com/review/create-review?asin=9334287195

It only takes a minute, and means a great deal to an independent author.